AFRICENTRIC CHRISTIANITY

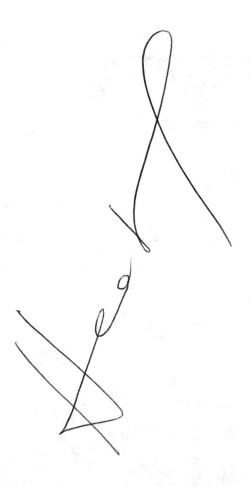

AFRICENTRIC CHRISTIANITY
A THEOLOGICAL APPRAISAL FOR MINISTRY

J. DEOTIS ROBERTS

Judson Press

Valley Forge

Africentric Christianity: A Theological Appraisal for Ministry
© 2000 by Judson Press, Valley Forge, PA 19482-0851
All rights reserved.

Bible quotations in this volume are from *The Holy Bible*, King James Version.

Library of Congress Cataloging-in-Publication Data
Roberts, J. Deotis (James Deotis), 1927–
    Africentric Christianity : a theological appraisal for ministry / J. Deotis Roberts.
        p. cm.
    Includes bibliographical references.
    ISBN 0-8170-1321-0 (pbk. : alk. paper)
    1. Afro-Americans—Religion. 2. Afrocentrism—Religious aspects—Christianity.
3. Black theology. I. Title.
BR563.N4R6 2000
230'.089'96073–dc21   99-32820

Printed in the U.S.A.
06 05 04 03 02 01 00
10 9 8 7 6 5 4 3 2 1

Contents

Preface

THE AFRICAN AMERICAN COMMUNITY has taken a quarter century to focus on the search for our African heritage. The quest for heritage is a constant. Africentrism, a historical and cultural perspective for people of African ancestry, has gained a popularity and respectability that the black power movement was not able to achieve. Some middle-class blacks were never able to accept their blackness, perhaps because the positive meaning of the designation was never apparent to them. Some Europeanized African Americans still seem hesitant to accept their links to Africa. However, the Africentric outlook is gaining ground in many circles.

The word "Afrocentric" has currency in a wide range of activities and events among African Americans, and the word "Africentric," now often used instead of the word "Afrocentric," seems to be gaining ground because of the former's more etymologically correct connection to its root, "Africa." Philadelphia is filled with Africentrism. Professor Molefi Asante at Temple University, the architect of the idea of Africentrism, is friendly with ministers and churches. People are asking what the concept means. Most pastors instinctively embrace the notion, since it is part of the search for roots in the African American community. It can be viewed in popular festivals and entertainment, in family reunions, in educational circles, and in church and community activities. Public school teachers in urban America are attending workshops on the subject of Africentrism and teaching it in our schools. Some African Americans are taking educational tours to Africa, especially to Egypt, the mother country.

Unfortunately, the profound message inherent in the concept is seldom explored. If the movement is worthy and is to be more than a fad, then a serious effort must be undertaken to explain its meaning and message. No one person can be responsible for such an awesome task.

Africentrism is more than wearing African garments or dancing to percussive African music. It involves more than a cultural revival.

It requires a new perspective of life, a cultural conversion. It leads to a new life view and worldview for African peoples. Africentrism builds upon the self-respect and empowerment aspects of the black consciousness–black power movement, the emphasis on blackness that gave rise to black studies, including black church studies and black theology. Africentric leaders give due credit to the contributions of persons such as Martin Luther King Jr. and Malcolm X. Unlike the black power movement, Africentrism seeks to reinterpret our history and reconstruct our culture. It does not rest with slavery or with our ancestry in West Africa; it takes us back to classical African history in Ethiopia and especially Egypt.

Africentrism deconstructs much of Western classical history, re-claiming Egypt for Africa and challenging the hegemony of ancient Greece. This reinterpretation and reconstruction has profound impli-cations for a new view of classical philosophy and culture. Persons like myself who have read and researched classical thought and the church tradition in the West are challenged to do much rethinking regarding the Western bias of our history of ideas that has shaped theological thinking for thousands of years. Our black biblical schol-ars, led by Cain Hope Felder, have taken the lead in rethinking biblical sources and interpretation from an Africentric point of view.

If Africentrism is taught and practiced in school and the wider community, we need to be aware that it is coming into our churches. We need to have more than a superficial understanding of the con-cept. We need to critically examine it and seek to determine what aspects of the idea can be compatible with the Christian faith. The time has come for a critical theological appraisal of this powerful notion. As a minister-theologian with a philosophical orientation, I am committed to the academy and the church, especially to theo-logical teaching and education. From this vantage point, I seek to provide a theological assessment of the Africentric outlook by exam-ining the scholarship that has brought the concept to our attention. My ultimate agenda is an appraisal of Africentrism for the church. In this theological appraisal of Africentrism, a number of issues are addressed: Is it possible to be Africentric and a devout Christian at the same time? Is it possible to enrich and empower the witness and mission of black churches through the Africentric perspective? If one becomes thoroughly Africentric, is it possible to affirm the humanity of all people and witness to all people in an ecumenical and pluralistic climate? Of what use is Africentrism as a cultural medium to convey the Christian message of redemption and witness? Will Africentrism help black Christians to communicate and express their faith in a multicultural social environment? These are only some of the issues considered in this study. I do not promise to provide conclusive answers to all the issues we face, but I intend to stimulate serious reflection. This may lead to the breakthrough we need on this vital subject.

The concept of Africentrism is useful for enhancing our sense of worth as persons and as a people among other groups. The concept can be used inclusively as well as exclusively. To affirm one's own heritage does not necessitate the denigration of the heritage of others.

In life as in thought, one can see only what one is prepared to see. How one interprets or is prepared to interpret experience determines to a large degree the meaning it conveys to us. I have made two visits to Egypt. The first visit was by way of Asia and the Middle East. I was traveling to seek to understand non-Christian religions. Prior to my study tour, I had studied and taught these religions for several years. My outlook was focused on my mission as a historian of religion. I had encountered Islam in India and Pakistan, and now I was to view it in Lebanon, Jordan, Turkey, and Egypt. Arabic is the national language and Islam the major religion I encountered in the Egyptian experience. Although it was a powerful learning experience, it was limited by my focus and what I was prepared to see.

A second visit to Egypt was different. I arrived in Egypt after ten days in the heart of sub-Saharan Africa. Representative countries of West, Central, and East Africa were on my itinerary. I was seeking to learn more about traditional African life and the culture and religion associated with this tradition. Again, I was seeking to look at the situation more as a philosopher of religion than as a theologian. I must admit my commitment to theology went with me. I took several side trips to observe Christian faith and practices informed by traditional African beliefs. On the whole I was attempting to understand my African heritage better.

On this latter study tour, I entered Egypt by way of Ethiopia. This point of entrance gave me a sense of Egypt's relation to the continent of Africa. My encounter with black Israelites and Ethiopian

Orthodox Christians was important. Even though my guide in Egypt was an Islamic scholar, I saw an affinity with Africa that I had not previously observed. We looked at Coptic Christianity in an illuminating way. The people look much like those in the other African countries I had visited. Questions regarding Eurocentric scholarship crowded by mind. It seemed so obvious that Egypt is an African country, and much of what I had studied was severely questioned.

After an intense study of Africentrism, I am prepared for a third visit. I am now prepared to see, hear, and learn in something of a different order. My experiences are presented to illustrate the point stated earlier, that we see what we are prepared to see and learn.

Felder produced a moving videotape in Israel with the assistance of the department of communications at Howard University. He identified with the community of black Israelites in that country. His Africentric biblical scholarship prepared him to see and understand what many biblical scholars have never seen. Western scholars with a limited mindset may make frequent visits to Israel, but they are blind to the knowledge that Felder has so movingly shared with his colleagues. Felder's experience in Israel was informed by Africentric reflections on the Bible. I allude to Felder's and my experiences in order to illustrate the point I stated at the outset: what one sees is informed by what one is prepared to see and learn.

Chapter 1 is concerned with the importance of Africentrism for the African American church tradition. This chapter sets the stage for what is to follow in the remainder of the book.

Chapter 2 attempts to present the Africentric outlook on black history by focusing on the classical roots of that history in Egypt, Ethiopia, and Nubia. In doing so, I wish to reclaim all African history, insisting that Egypt is a part of Africa and therefore important for the self-understanding of all African peoples.

Chapter 3 looks at the history discussed in chapter 2 from the contemporary Africentric perspective. Additional information is provided in order to place the Africentric idea in a meaningful context. This chapter also recognizes the perspective that African American women theologians have brought to the Africentric discussion.

Chapter 4 is concerned with the use of Africentric perspective in biblical interpretation. I compare the liberation motif of biblical interpretation and the Africentric hermeneutic of Felder and others.

Chapter 5 revisits the discussion of the Black Messiah embraced during the early years of black theology. The chapter includes a careful look at the critique provided by womanist theologian Kelly Brown Douglas. Finally, I will apply the insights of the Africentric perspective to an updated version of the concept.

Chapter 6 concerns the African American understanding of God as Creator, Redeemer, and Sanctifier, which comes out of the African American understanding of oppression. The chapter presents a trinitarian understanding of God in Africentric perspective.

Beginning with **chapter 7,** drawing on my own experiences and observations, I turn my theological appraisal toward some suggestions appropriate for the philosophy, development, and practice of church ministry. I attempt to indicate how the Africentric outlook has both a priestly and prophetic relevance for ministry in the black church.

Chapter 8 delves into multiple dimensions of worship. Here I discuss how our African heritage and culture contribute to music, drama, dance, preaching, rites of passage, family reunions, and other areas of worship.

Chapter 9 suggests ways that the Africentric outlook can contribute to our ministry of people's social needs and comments on the importance of the strong family values of our heritage.

Chapter 10 takes up the mission of the black church in this time of multiculturalism. I explore the effectiveness of the Africentric outlook in the setting of a cross-cultural witness of Christians with many different ethnic backgrounds.

As professor at Eastern Baptist Theological Seminary in Philadelphia, I was challenged to serious reflection on Africentrism. Asante has stimulated much thought and action around the Africentric idea in churches, community activities, and educational institutions in Philadelphia. Black Clergy, Inc. has taken up the concept and urged seminaries to include this perspective in educating church leadership. Beyond this, Asante and I have had a personal dialogue in private and in public. He has shared with me a great deal of unpublished material, key articles, and essays of his wide discussions with proponents and opponents of his viewpoint.

My wife, Elizabeth, now retired, has taught elementary classes in the District of Columbia for more than thirty years. She has taken workshops on Africentrism and used her exposure to this idea in her instruction and class activities. I have gained much from her in estimating the educational use of Africentrism.

During a three-year period, I have had the privilege of sharing my ideas on Africentrism in several contexts. I gained much insight and encouragement from lectures at the University of The South, Shaw University, Memphis Theological Seminary, and Maryland United Baptist Seminary and College, to name a few occasions.

I wish to acknowledge the input of my students at Yale Divinity School and Eastern Baptist Theological Seminary. A visiting professorship at Duke University Divinity School has been important in the final development of this work. Dean L. Gregory Jones, Associate Dean Willie Jennings, and my student assistants, Prince Rivers and William Lamar, and students in my seminars, among others, have aided me greatly in working toward my goal.

A generous grant from the Louisville Institute during the 1997–98 academic year made the extra research for this study and manuscript preparation possible. I owe the institute a debt of gratitude.

Too, I appreciate the quality work of the editors at Judson Press, whose efforts greatly improved the text of the manuscript. In particular, my thanks go to Randy Frame, acquisition editor at Judson, who worked closely with me to see this project through to its completion.

While my youngest daughter, Kristina, has contributed to the research and word processing of this manuscript, other members of my family have supported me in additional ways. My wife, Elizabeth, and my other two daughters, Carlita Rose Marsh and Charmaine Parker, together with my grandchildren, have supported my effort through their tolerance of my absence and through their abiding love.

Although I acknowledge the assistance of many persons in this effort, I personally accept its shortcomings. I will, however, be greatly rewarded if other able scholars take up the task and share their insights for the good of our common future.

J. D. R.
Duke Divinity School
Spring 2000

Chapter I

What Is Africentrism?

I N A CONFERENCE ON AFROCENTRISM at Temple University in 1994, the statement of a former Princeton Theological seminarian stunned me.[1] He was an ex-Christian who had replaced Christianity with Afrocentrism. and considered Africa rather than Israel as the Holy Land for African Americans seeking holy places. He chided black Christians for flying over the sacred shrines of their African ancestors in search of a proper destination to enrich their faith.

For this "true believer" Africentrism was a substitute for the Christian faith, and his introduction to this new idea was in the nature of religious conversion. This confession seems unique and does not appear to accurately represent the outlook of Molefi Asante and other leaders of the Africentric movement. In fact chief exponents of Africentrism are somewhat ambivalent and noncommittal at this point. They appear to prefer dialogue instead of confrontation with Christian leaders.

It is timely, nevertheless, for Christian theologians to seek an in-depth understanding of the Africentric movement. The place to begin is to seek to understand Asante, who stands at the fountainhead of the movement.

Asante: The Man

One of sixteen children, Molefi Kete Asante was born in Valdosta, Georgia. His grandfather was a minister, and he was also a preacher in early life. He studied at UCLA, where he headed the Student Non-violent Coordinating Committee (SNCC) in the 1960s. At the age of twenty-six he was awarded a doctoral degree by UCLA, and at thirty he became a full professor at the State University of New York at Buffalo.

1

His study and field experience in Africa is extensive. Asante is a mature Africanist who has acquired knowledge of the languages, cultures, and philosophies of that vast continent. He trained journalists in Zimbabwe. On May 28, 1994, he was recognized by the Ghanaian royal court, the first such honor bestowed upon an African American. Crowned with the title "Royal Commander of the Last Battalion," he was considered a person with commitment to the well-being of African people in the United States and Africa.

As a scholar Asante founded the Africentric movement. Under his name the concept of Africentricity has been established in educational, cultural, and religious circles. As professor and chair of the department of African American Studies at Temple University, Asante created the first department of its kind in the nation.

A well-known writer, Asante has produced more than thirty-seven books and some two hundred articles and essays. He has coauthored and coedited other works. With a close colleague, Abu S. Abarry, Asante has recently released a book of sources, a magisterial work titled *African Intellectual Heritage*. An intellectual activist, Asante founded the *Journal of Black Studies* and the National Afrocentric Institute. Each year the Diop Conference is held at Temple in honor of Asante's main African mentor, the African scholar Cheikh Auta Diop.

Asante's activities and influence have spread nationally and internationally through his initiatives. He is known through his use of the mass media, having appeared on *Nightline*, BET, and other outlets. *The Today Show, The Tony Brown Show,* and *Night Watch* have featured him.

He has served as an educational consultant for school districts in Detroit, New York, Baltimore, Camden, Cleveland, the Virgin Islands, New Orleans, Gary, Indiana, and elsewhere. He conducts study tours to Egypt and Ethiopia and other areas of classical Africa on a frequent basis. This is one means by which his scholarship comes alive for leaders who desire an in-depth immersion in the Africentric experience.

Asante's message has had a powerful influence upon black churches. One can especially observe the perspective at work among African American churches in Philadelphia. I first encountered Asante's message to the churches and seminaries in a Fall Convocation at Howard Divinity School. Asante was in conversation with Dr. Cain Hope Felder, Dr. Cheryl Sanders, and others. His moving sermon-address in that setting was at once a message of encouragement and tremendous challenge for theologians, pastors, and laity.

In Philadelphia, the theological seminaries in collaboration with Black Clergy, Inc. have added to their studies a continuing education component out of the Africentric perspective. As a former member of the education committee of Black Clergy, I have been greatly involved in drafting an Africentric statement, planning and teaching a section of this Africentric theological enrichment/empowerment program.

On two occasions I have been in dialogue with Asante in a public form at Eastern Baptist Theological Seminary. I have been with him in the context of worship at Canaan Baptist Church, where he delivered the morning message. He is very much at home in the black pulpit. In my view a deep understanding of Africentrism is a precondition for a careful appraisal of the outlook. On that basis I will be able to do a more responsible critique of the concept for use in the Christian movement. In my *Philosophical Introduction to Theology,* I attempted a historical critique of various ideological systems in the West and their use in the understanding of the Christian faith. Much of this hindsight is used in my evaluation of the Africentric idea.

Asante: The Message[2]

Asante's views are based upon works of several predecessors. *Africentricity* is a dynamic intellectual theory, not a *system* of thought but a philosophical and theoretical *perspective*. In the Africentric view the problem of *location* takes precedence over the topic under consideration. Africentrists argue that Africans have been moved off of social, political, philosophical, and economic terms in most discourse in the West for more than five hundred years. Due to European influence, for instance, references to classical music, theater, or dance are usually references to European music, theater, and dance. Europe occupies all the intellectual and artistic seats in these areas of knowledge. According to the Africentric appraisal of this situation, no room is left for other traditions. Similarly, a department of modern languages refers to European languages. Asian and African languages are not considered.

Africentrists seize the opportunity to reinterpret Europeanized writings of early Africans in Africa and in the Americas. Literary interpretation is based on location, which can be manifest in psychological, cultural, economic, social, and other forms. By identifying elements in a text that reveal an author's personal location, one is able to interpret a text in the language of Africentricity. The notable aspects of a textual and personal location are observed from the attitude, direction, and language of the text. Thus it is possible to determine location, dislocation, and relocation by observing the centeredness of a text.

In Africentric analyses the relation of subject to data is a critical tool for assessing location. In the Eurocentric perspective the relationship of the European subject to data assumes a normative universal status. The aggrandizement of Eurocentrism renders Africa as an object rather than a subject. The Africentric movement stresses "African agency," a growing intellectual idea that surfaced in the 1980s as many African and African American scholars adopted an Africentric orientation. Africentrists maintain that the only way to understand African literary or dramatic expression is by examining all data from the standpoint of Africans as subjects, as human agents rather than as objects in a European frame of reference. Africentricity is opposed to theories that *dislocate* Africans to the periphery of human thought and experience. It has implications for fields as different as dance, economics, social work, literature, politics, psychology, philosophy, and religion.

A contradiction between history and intellectual perspective produces a kind of incongruity called *decenteredness*. For instance, when an African American writes from the viewpoint of Europeans who came to the Americas on the *Mayflower,* or when literary critics write of Africans as "the other," Africentrists claim that Africans are being marginalized — sometimes even by Africans themselves. Continental Africans who accept David Livingstone's naming of *Musi wa Tunya* as Victoria Falls are *dislocated.* In this situation, Africentrists call for a *recentering* or *relocating* of Africans in an *agent* position.

The matter of culture must be addressed. Human beings cannot divest themselves of culture; they participate either in their own historical culture or in that of some other group. One can participate in a multiplicity of cultural locations, but it is essential that one participate in culture as such. Africentrists question certain usages that tend to be Eurocentric with universal implications. Usually "the Continent" refers to Europe, but Africa is also a continent. In reference to Africa the term needs to be recentered in a human context that allows for intellectual space to be shared by all human and cultural agents.

Africentrists accept the multiplicity of cultural centers and therefore do not negate Eurocentrism except where Eurocentrism promotes itself as universal. Africentrists are open to those of European backgrounds to fully express their culture. They should use literary allusions, illustrations, and figures that emerge from their cultural center. At the same time they should encourage the similar expressions by those who come from other cultural contexts.

In order to be *centered* one needs to be located as an agent instead of as "the other." Metaphors of location and dislocation are the principle tools of analysis, because events, situations, texts, phenomena, and authors display various levels of centeredness. Thus we are faced with a critical shift in thinking. The Africentric perspective provides new insights and dimensions to the understanding of texts and phenomena.

According to Asante, Africentricity has a psychological dimension. For example, psychological *misorientation* or *disorientation* may characterize our attitudes as African people when we consider ourselves to be Europeans or believe that it is impossible to be simultaneously African and human. An African centeredness can be helpful toward self-pride and people affirmation. This positive outlook can have educative value and can lead to a wholesome revision of the American educational curriculum.

An Africentric Worldview

Asante sees that if we do not intelligently and boldly place Africa at the center of our "existential reality," those who see Europe as their center constantly misunderstand us. We become isolated and spiritually lonely as a people within the African diaspora. Anti-Africa rhetoric and symbols constantly beset us.[3] Asante correctly assumes that some African Americans are guided by an education that alienates them from Africa:

Unable to call the power of ancestors, because one does not know them, without an ideology of heritage, because one does not respect one's own prophets, the person is like an ant trying to move a large piece of garbage only to find that it will not move.[4]

Asante's main academic discipline is rhetoric. Knowledge of his concern about the use of language is essential if one is to follow his line of thought. He criticizes blacks who become Muslims. They learn Arabic in order to read the Qur'an and assume Islamic names. They make the trip to Mecca. On their way to Mecca they fly over many sacred cities and sites in Africa in order to march around someone else's sacred stone.

Asante insists, "If your God cannot speak to you in your language, then he is not your God."[5] He encourages African Americans to embrace Ebonico,[6] Yoruba, Asante, Twi, or another similar language. We should seek to hear God in the language of our ancestors. African Americans should also honor their holy places, such as Lake Bosumtwi, where the God of Africa dwells. The place of Nat Turner's revolt in Virginia is holy ground. We have many such places comparable to any sacred places on earth. Africentrism directs us to visit and meditate at these sites.

Asante moves deeper into his critique of religious choices of African Americans. He asserts that to embrace a religion is to anchor oneself into the culture out of which the original religion emerged. Religion needs to be carefully selected, for it is the most powerful tool of mind control ever created.[7] His criticism of accepting Islam is applied to Christianity. He writes: "The most crippling effect of Islam as well as Christianity for us may well be the adoption of non-African customs and behaviors."[8] Marxism as an ideology is no less to be shunned.

For Asante Africentricity is like a religious conversion experience. He compares one's movement into this new outlook with the acceptance of Jesus Christ as Savior: "Old things pass away and all things become new."[9] He does not advocate hatred for other religions or cultures. Instead he urges us to cling to our African heritage. Our roots go back to East Africa. We do not find the Hebrews until thousands of years after the ancient Egyptians (Africans) and Nubians (Africans) had appeared. The African continent gave birth to Africans. Africentricity is our destiny as African people:

[Afrocentricity] a new perspective; a new approach, a new consciousness invades our behavior and consequently with Afrocentricity ... you see other people differently, you read books differently, you see politicians differently, in fact, nothing is as it was before your consciousness. Your conversion to Afrocentricity becomes total as you read, listen, and talk with others who share the collective consciousness. It supersedes any other ideology because it is the proper sanctification of your history.[10]

Asante mentions Islam, Christianity, Buddhism, and Judaism among religions and also notes the ideology of Marxism. For him Africentricity can stand its ground against any ideology or religion. "As a people, our most cherished and valuable achievements are the achievements of spirit. With an Afrocentric spirit, all things can be made to happen; it is the source of genuine revolutionary commitment."[11]

He places the Africentric perspective on a pedestal, like a religious conversion. It is a substitute for any religion or ideology. Yet it is a cultural phenomenon. Some questions beg for answers: Are culture and religion identical? Is any cultural-historical situation coterminous with religion? Christians would disagree, and so would Muslims. What about the prophetic dimension of religion? Religions often stand over against cultures in critical judgment due to a transcendent norm inherent in a religion. What about salvific needs of sinful human beings? Are ancestors, even African ancestors, able to forgive sins and reconcile us to the divine? Does the ability to use a cultural language and call gods by name in these languages provide any assurance that these gods can hear us and also redeem?

Africentricity and the African American Tradition

To his credit Asante does not ignore the contribution of black leaders of the past. Many of the leaders discussed would not agree with his total outlook, but Asante credits them for paving the way for his perspective. Although he pays tribute to the forefathers among our ancestors, he gives little attention to our foremothers.[12] A noble procession of African American leaders is discussed. Among these are Booker T. Washington, Marcus Garvey, Martin Luther King Jr., Elijah Muhammad, W. E. B. DuBois, and Malcolm X. Among these leaders Malcolm seems to emerge at a superior level.

Asante views Malcolm X as an activist and commentator on the revolutionary road to an Africentric viewpoint. Malcolm inspired many subsequent ideologies and thinkers toward our liberation. Malcolm's philosophy was rich and powerful. It generated a thousand ways to fight for freedom. However, according to Asante, Malcolm himself did not reach the Africentric stance.[13]

The Meaning of Africentrism

Asante argues for a practical project. Africentricity is not the mere existence of an "African Person." It is the active, self-conscious, humanizing motif in every sector of society. It must inform architecture, economics, and political science and must effect dynamic change. According to Asante, being black does not make one Africentric. While he sees Africentrism as building upon several foundations, such as Garveyism and *Négritude,* it reaches beyond these foundations. It is African people immersing themselves in a cultural rebirth, the only path toward the liberation of our children and ourselves.[14]

Africentrism is not a fad or something external; it is internal and requires dedication of thought and action. An experience of mine serves as an illustration. I met a young black man at the Lagos airport as I entered Nigeria in 1971. After much difficulty we were cleared by passport control to enter Nigeria. This young man from Harlem was fully dressed in African attire. It soon became apparent that he was not financially prepared for his trip. He asked to share a taxi with me. On the way to downtown Lagos, he indicated that he would like to share a room for one night. My compassion moved me to rent a twin-bed room for one night. He insisted that he wanted to head for "the bush" the next day. Though I was tired from travel, I did not sleep that night — I did not trust my roommate. He did leave the next day. Within a few days I met him again. He was overcome by culture shock and was on the way to the airport to return home. This experience illustrated the difference between my sense of mission and a visit to Africa based upon some romantic notion of return "to the homeland." This obviously would not meet the test of the type of Africentric orientation Asante intends.

Hundreds of years separate African Americans in this country and the African experience in tribal and village life. Here was a young black man who was moved by his experience in Harlem. He may have seen Alex Haley's *Roots* and even participated in the upheavals in the late 1960s. He was not prepared intellectually, culturally, ideologically, or otherwise for the cultural shock he faced in the village he visited. With careful study and much more experience, I did not rush into the village. Urban life was for me a halfway experience. Lagos was cosmopolitan — it was similar to our city life. People I met took me into the villages and explained life and customs. In this way I was able to gradually enter into a deeper understanding of village life in Nigeria. Asante urges those who would be Africentric to study and grow into a profound understanding of an Africentered outlook.

Our intellectual struggle centers upon the rejection of European particularism as universal. Five hundred years of propaganda, cultural exploitation, distorted information, and physical annihilation have left us denuded of our true heritage. Thousands of years of African civilization have disappeared from our minds and psyches. Our minds are locked in theoretical, political, economic and cultural chains, and the most difficult task before people of African descent is to liberate their minds. For Asante, the goal of Africentricity is what he calls a "cultural project" — to restore an appreciation for our culture, reclaim our history, and put a stop to our intellectual and cultural disfranchisement.[15]

> The Afrocentric cultural project is a holistic plan to reconstruct and develop every dimension of the African world from the standpoint of Africa as subject rather than object.... Afrocentricity assumes the African government officials will become conscious of the centrality of Africa in their deliberations, that writers will seek to influence the African people, that we re-connect in our minds, ancient Nubia and Kemet to the rest of Africa, that we speak on every subject and every issue affecting the world.[16]

Asante has Pan-African perspectives. From my personal experiences, I see a great need for his message to take root on the continent of Africa as well as in the African diaspora. He sees the task of Africans overseas to reclaim their ancient heritage and live by its values and principles. African people are disconnected and scattered around the globe. We are also confused regarding our identity. Often we have assumed new identities and become doubly lost. For instance, some African Americans have become zombies in the midst of the stone and steel cities of the world. Asante speaks in direct language

concerning this situation: "It is imperative that Africans in Columbia who speak Spanish, the Africans in Brazil who speak Portuguese,
the Africans in Martinique who speak French, and the Africans in
Jamaica who speak English be brought into this cultural project."[17]

The concern for African unity should also include Africans on
the continent. Cultural and tribal conflicts in Africa are divisive. All
Africans have been victimized by some form of oppression — slavery,
racism, or colonialism. The scars from these forms of victimization
are deep in the psyche and collective unconsciousness. These patholo-
gies have been internalized, and we have often made our own people
the oppressed of the oppressed.

Asante compares this need to overcome alien cultural activity to
those who seem to have dealt with this condition. He points to
Australian Europeans living thousands of miles from Europe to participate in the European project. In like manner, Africans must be a
part of the cultural project in Cuba, the United States, Haiti, Nic-
aragua, or Mexico.[18] The task is formidable, but it is possible and
necessary. There follows this summons: "Let the artist imagine, let
the scientist expand, let the priests see visions, let the writers be free
to create, and let the Afrocentric revolution be born!"[19]

Collective Consciousness

An important concern for assuming the Africentric perspective is "collective consciousness." Without this type of awareness we cannot
obtain unity. Asante's thinks that for African Americans, who are
beginning to come to terms with America, this collective consciousness is on the upsurge. This consciousness was already present during
the nineteenth century among some black leaders.

Among the nineteenth-century leaders were Paul Cuffee, Edward
Blyden, Marcus Garvey, Henry McNeal Turner, and Harriet Tubman.
Though it is good for persons of stature to search for the essence of
the African soul, we must now reach the masses with this challenge.
According to Asante, such collective consciousness is a prerequisite
for coming together as a people. Malcolm X was against integration
because he saw it as an attempt to absorb black culture into white
culture. We need to be able to affirm the value of black culture out
of the Africentric orientation.[20]

Consciousness is more than a mere acceptance. It requires psychological and political action. Asante discusses the notion of the "predicament of consciousness," our responses to external forces in our social context. Asante observes that we must be aware of our presence in a racist, hostile, and alien type of situation. We must be prepared to deal with negative verbal encounters and say what needs to be said, be who we must be, and write what we must, in order to keep and extend our sanity. Our consciousness also needs to constantly expand. Our responses must be based upon vigilance and positive assertions to counteract the erosion of our consciousness. We need to be mindful of the way we are being treated in films and the mass media. Asante states his case as follows: "Once we have entertained the ideas of consciousness, mulled them over, accepted the concept of Pan-Americanism, related our Africentricity to Africa and the Diaspora, and made terms with our ancestors, we will have dealt successfully with the predicament of consciousness."[21]

In order to understand fully that the core of our collective being is African, we must recall our history. Regardless of our skin color or degrees of consciousness, we are by virtue of commitments, history, and convictions[22] an African people. Africentrism is a philosophical outlook determined by our history.

Although a great deal of emphasis is placed upon collective awareness, Asante also views individual awareness as the entrance for a full Africentric collective consciousness. At this point he sees the *Négritude* movement as a background movement. This movement based in French-speaking African countries has real importance.[23] We need to dislodge ourselves from slave names, according to Asante. We are victims of our names, since our use of such names is a refusal to assert that we are an African people.

What's in a Name?

Asante views the assumption of African names as a great advance toward a collective consciousness. Our struggle in naming who we are as a people is related to both self-identification and collective consciousness. The struggle is illustrated in various designations we have used for ourselves: African, Afro-American, black, Negro, colored, and African American. Regardless of what we call ourselves, in order to be authentic we need to be aware that we are an African people.

Asante applauds the trend of young parents who are giving their children African names. Freed slaves chose names they had heard from whites, often from their masters, and consequently most of them had slave names. Upon taking on these names, they became bodies without spirit and people without dignity, whether they knew it or not.

"What changes with the changing of our names is how we perceive ourselves, and how others perceive us. Changing of names will not in itself change economic and social oppression, but it will contribute to the creation of new economic, political and social forces that anticipate change. The name-changing action is at once a rejection and an acceptance, a necessary condition for a new perspective on our place in the world."[24]

Asante urges us to assume African names in the same way that Christians take Christian names and Muslims Arabic names. As long as we retain slave names, we carry on the trappings of slavery. We are our own worst enemies, being tied to white cultural, historical, and symbolic systems. He observes that whites had never had to react to us apart from slavery. We have seldom confronted that history ourselves; when we do, we'll initiate our liberation. Dignity must be accepted, and acceptance depends upon consciousness of who we are. Only African names reflect the proper consciousness. Assuming an African name allows us to participate in the collective consciousness of Africentricity.[25]

Epistemological Critique
of European American Thought

Critical theory is popular among Asante's colleagues in philosophy and religion at Temple University. Therefore, Asante quite naturally aims his critique of Eurocentric thought at the Frankfurt School. He promises a radical critique of Eurocentric ideology that claims to be universal. In his approach, Africa is *subject* and not *object*. He observes that the inability to see from several angles is a common fallacy in provincial scholarship.[26]

Asante is saying that the claim Eurocentrists make of "universal hegemony" is false.[27] Over against Asante's criticism of Eurocentrism, he presents a "metatheory" known as "Afrology." Afrology is in fact "Africentricity," the theory of social change. It denotes the study of African concepts, issues, and behaviors and includes research on African themes in the Americas, the West Indies, and the African continent.

He presents some of the characteristics of this Africentric outlook. Three are worthy of attention: First, there is the interrelatedness of thinking, feeling, and willing. "Human beings tend to recognize three fundamental existential postures...feeling, knowing, and acting. Afrology recognizes these three stances as interrelated, not separate."[28]

Second, in this metatheory the concept of *nommo* is used for African communication. He examines African American oratory as the totalization of the Africentric perspective. *Nommo* is "the generative and productive power of the spoken word." In brief, *nommo* is "word-force."[29]

Third, *orature* is the total body of oral discourses, styles, and traditions of African people.[30] It refers to such oral expressions as drumming, storytelling, praise, singing, dancing, and naming. The drum has a special function in African cultures. It is an awesome means of communication in African societies. The message sent by drum was swift and wide-ranging. The first drummer would reach as many people as possible. When he reached his full range, another drummer would take up the message. "The drummer, along with the village sage, became a repository of all the necessary historical data relating to the village."[31]

By way of making a clear distinction between the Africentric and the Eurocentric perspectives, Asante sets the "Afro-circular" view over against the "Euro-linear" view. The "Euro-linear" view seeks to predict and control; the "Afro-circular" view seeks to interpret and understand. A plurality of vision is created as persons from different cultures meet. Our capacity to see is culturally conditioned.[32]

Conclusion

An understanding of the person and message of Asante is basic to any serious encounter or evaluation of the Africentric perspective.

This chapter treats only provisionally the vast outlay of material on Asante's Africentric project.

From the sources Asante suggests best represent his message,[33] we can outline certain basic assumptions. A convenient summary of his Africentric proposal may be stated as follows:

1. We need to begin our cultural view of Africa with a study of Egypt, Nubia, Cush, and other ancient African cultures.

2. We need to be Africa-oriented in our study of data; Africa becomes subject rather than object. We recenter and relocate Africa as subject.

3. We need to lay claim to our own culture. We cannot divest ourselves of culture. We will either participate in our own culture or the culture of someone else.

4. Africentrists accept the multiplicity of cultural centers. They do not negate Eurocentrism except when Eurocentrism promotes itself as universal.

5. One is to accept the Africentric outlook as a means for both belief and practice.

For Asante the Africentric perspective is not only a proposal but also a project. As a scholar-activist, from student days to the present he has sparked a movement. Based at Temple University, he has surrounded himself with a group of like-minded scholars from Africa and the African diaspora.

Like any innovative movement, Africentrism could easily become a fad without substantive meaning. If Africentrism were no more than a fad, serious reflection upon its meaning for the Christian faith or for black churches would be a wasted effort.

As the term clearly implies, Africentrism is a way of viewing reality other than from a Eurocentric outlook. It entails a serious attempt to understand the manner in which Africans have viewed reality in their context of culture for thousands of years before they encountered the Western worldview. African Americans attempt to recover their classical roots through empathy, knowledge, and experience. Through new looking glasses, we peer into this Africentered world to observe what may be useful in our commitment to Christianity. What is useful? What must be rejected? What will enrich and empower our Christian way of life?

Having looked at Asante's proposal, which is representative of the Africentric movement, we can now put this Africentered focus in historical perspective. In a real sense "who we are is who we were!" Our past is an index to our future as a people. Looking back, we also look forward as we take our place among the peoples of the world.

Notes

1. At the Diop Conference at Temple University, 1995.

2. Besides drawing on my personal dialogue with Asante, I have used several basic sources: *The Afrocentric Idea* (Philadelphia: Temple University Press, 1987), *Afrocentricity* (Trenton, N.J.: Third World Press, 1988), and, *Kemet, Afrocentricity and Knowledge* (Trenton, N.J.: Third World Press, 1992). Among his shorter reports are "Afrocentric Systematics," *Black Issues in Higher Education* (August 13, 1992), 16–22.

3. *Afrocentricity*, rev. ed. (Trenton, N.J.: Africa World Press, 1988).

4. Ibid., 1.

5. Ibid., 2.

6. Ebonics uses many English words, but it is based on African syntactic elements and sense of modalities. Ibid., 121.

7. Ibid., 5.

8. Ibid.

9. Ibid., 7.

10. Ibid.

11. Ibid., 43.

12. Asante speaks of Harriet Tubman in glowing terms in *The Afrocentric Idea*, 102–5. She is called "The Great Mother" (105).

13. *Afrocentricity*, 19. Asante has high regards for Malcolm X's speech and action. See his *Malcolm X as Cultural Hero* (Trenton, N.J.: Africa World Press, 1993), chap. 4.

14. *Afrocentricity*, 104.

15. Ibid., 104–5.

16. Ibid., 105.

17. Ibid., 106.

18. Ibid.

19. Ibid., 107.

20. Ibid., 28.

21. Ibid., 28.

22. Ibid., 27.

23. Ibid., 69–70.

24. Ibid., 28.

25. Ibid., 28–29. Cf. 71–78, where he looks at the Akan naming tradition.

26. *The Afrocentric Idea*, 3.

27. Ibid., 4.
28. Ibid., 16–17.
29. Ibid., 17–18.
30. Ibid., 60.
31. Ibid., 59.
32. Ibid., 71–78.
33. The three books he suggests as being foundational for the Afrocentric project are *Afrocentricity, The Afrocentric Idea,* and *Kemet, Afrocentricity and Knowledge.* This chapter has stressed the first two volumes. *Kemet,* it appears, will be useful in the appraisal of his work in the historical context to follow.

Chapter 2

Afrocentrism/Africentrism in Historical Perspective

IN THIS CHAPTER I pursue theology through my experiences, an approach James W. McClendon has introduced as "biography as theology."[1] Although his approach is more objective than autobiographical, it allows for the self-understanding of the theologian to be brought into the account.

Steeped in the Western classical tradition of thought, as a student I was in pursuit of a responsible faith. My intellectual tools had been sharpened by study at Hartford, Edinburgh, and Cambridge. My first professorial position after earning my Ph.D. from Edinburgh University was at Howard, the most prestigious black institution of higher education in the nation and in the minds of many middle-class blacks "the black Harvard."

In my first systematic theology class was a group of raw recruits for ministry. Armed with much classical knowledge in philosophy and theology, I approached my charges with complete confidence, even though my age was in the same range as that of my students.

Soon after classes began, a young student from the Deep South raised his hand. He was bashful, his language unpolished, and he spoke with a hesitant voice. Nevertheless, his comments were penetrating. When he finished, my head was spinning. I was no longer the master of my subject. In essence, he said,

> I came from a small town down South. All I have known is suffering, poverty, and deprivation from the most brutish form of racism. My people share my experience. We are victims of racism at its worst. My call to ministry emerged out of this setting. I am here to study the Christian faith in order to comfort and deliver my people. I do not need to *prove* that God *exists*. I already *know* this. What I really want to know is "Does God care?"

This one question has remained with me and has haunted me for decades. It not only changed the context of that particular course; it redirected the type of theological reflection I have been involved in ever since. The implications of that question are the burden of this study.

Ideological Moments in Black History

As we seek to place Africentrism in historical context, we must look backward in order to look forward. In the movie *Amistad,* President Van Buren says, "If you don't know where you came from, you don't know who you are." This statement is very true for African Americans. Since our experience of oppression in the United States has been more like an exile than an exodus, we need a place to call home. Africa, as a symbolic home, serves this purpose for many African Americans.

Several ideological moments can be identified in our history. These moments, or paradigm shifts, have continuity. They are stations on the way to freedom or liberation for black people. They are not fads as some outside observers believe. This is why we are placing some emphasis upon self-understandings and people understandings during periods of black history that help us more fully understand the present and future.

Pan-Africanism

Pan-Africanism is a comprehensive ideology. The African American who thought and lived in this mode was W. E. B. DuBois, a scholar-activist par excellence. In the 1930s DuBois stated that "the Pan-African movement aimed at an intellectual understanding and co-operation among all groups of African descent in order to bring about the industrial and spiritual emancipation of the Negro people."[2] DuBois became a leader in the Pan-African movement and provides vivid accounts of proceedings and resolutions of the several Pan-African conferences. Therefore, he understood this movement from the inside as a participant-observer.

Pan-Africanism has been interpreted in a variety of ways, including self-government for African countries; economic, social and cultural development of the African continent; promotion of unity among

African states; the concept of an African personality or *Négritude;* and a movement of ideas and emotions.[3] Therefore, Pan-Africanism must be a comprehensive notion that includes people of African descent in global perspective — not merely Africans on the African continent but all Africans of the African diaspora. Thus, P. Olisanwuche Esedebe's concise definition is suitable:

> Pan-Africanism is a political and cultural phenomenon that regards Africa, Africans and African descendants abroad as a unit. It seeks to regenerate and unify Africa and promote a feeling of oneness among the people of the African world. It glorifies the African past and inculcates pride in African values. Any adequate definitions of the phenomenon must include the political and cultural aspects.[4]

In addition to the political and cultural aspects, the religious aspects must also be seriously considered. Otherwise, as this study shows in subsequent chapters, the meaning of Pan-Africanism is severely truncated.

Négritude

The *Négritude* movement, as the French name implies, is a form of "black consciousness." The spirit of *Négritude* is in DuBois's *Souls of Black Folk* and in Frantz Fanon's writings.

Aimé Césaire is one advocate of the concept of *Négritude.* He, like most of his colleagues in the movement, is from a French colonial territory, either in the West Indies or the African continent. Hailing from Martinique, he studied literature in Paris and later became mayor of Fort-de-France, capital of Martinique. He also was elected delegate to the Assembleé Nationale in Paris.

In order to understand Césaire's passion and outlook, we need to take a brief look at the island where he was born in 1913. Martinique, in the French West Indies, is a place of dazzling luxury and wealth on the part of a few, who are white, and a place of hunger, disease and ignorance, and abject poverty of the masses, who are black. The plight of blacks stems from former slavery and the exploitation that followed slavery.

Césaire uses the term *Négritude* when telling of an experience in Paris that was a turning point in his way of thinking about his blackness, his *Négritude*. He was on a Paris streetcar one evening when a homely, poorly dressed Negro was facing him. This hapless black became instantly the object of derision on the part of white passengers.

The black man was a misfit in this urban setting. His clothes were too large for him. He was large, but he tried to make himself small. He wanted to relax his gigantic legs. His fists were trembling with anxiety. His eyes were bloodshot and weary. He was an obvious victim of poverty. He was unshaven, with an arched back, panic-stricken — a hideous, ill-tempered, melancholy Negro. The white women behind Césaire saw the Negro as comical and ugly. They laughed openly and loudly as they looked at him.

Césaire's first response was to reassure himself that he had "nothing in common with that monkey." But he had to immediately reexamine his position as a black man in a white culture. It was necessary to reassess his whole racial philosophy and outlook. As a result, Césaire realized that his fate and that of the black in focus were inextricably linked. In spite of his French exterior, Césaire was also black and basically no different from the humblest, most ignorant, most ridiculous black. This realization was a turning point in his life. He declared, "I accept, I accept all that...Négritude" (*j'accepte, j'accepte tout cela...toute cette négritude;* Césaire, *Cahier d'un retour au pays natal*).[5]

This awareness essentially gave birth to the *Négritude* movement. Though anchored in the Afro-French writers from the 1930s, it has currency or meaning for blacks of African descent everywhere. Léopold Senghor, born Sengalese in 1906, was a notable member of this literary movement. Léon G. Damas was born in Cayenne, Guyana (French Guiana), South America, and studied in Martinique. However, he was to join Césaire and Senghor in Paris.

As a religious philosopher, I observe the mood of French existentialism in the *Négritude* outlook. It is an inward journey, but it also reflects an African collective consciousness. It cross-fertilized with similar concerns about the injustices of life under racist oppression of African Americans, some of whom were in conversation with *Négritude* writers in Paris. Its closest affinity with black writers appears in the literary output of the Harlem Renaissance. Edward A. Jones, professor of French and chair of the department of modern foreign languages at Morehouse College, sums up his understanding of the *Négritude* movement:

It may be said that the common denominator of all these writers is consciousness of color and racial pride, complemented by a deep conviction of solidarity among all Blacks, both in and outside Africa, who share a common heritage of oppression, injustice, poverty, and economic ills resulting therefrom.[6]

The Harlem Renaissance, or the "New Negro" Movement

At the same time that black awareness took place in Paris among black expatriates, a similar literary development occurred in the United States. Among the writers of the Harlem Renaissance were Charles W. Chesnutt, DuBois, Paul Laurence Dunbar, Claude McKay, Countée Cullen, and Langston Hughes. Novelists such as Jessie Fauset and Jean Toomer, artists Henry O. Tanner and William E. Scott, and sculptors such as Meta Warrick Fuller, Mae Jackson, and Elizabeth Prophet also emerged. Edward Jones observes a meeting of minds among these sons and daughters of Africa:

> The meetings [of *Négritude* exponents and the New Negro Movement] brought together Blacks from two hemispheres and facilitated cross-fertilization of talent, unity of purpose, and color solidarity. Common ancestry and background, community in suffering, and long-pent-up resentments bridged the geographical distance separating these sons [and daughters] of Africa and endowed them with a *cause commune*.[7]

The Harlem Renaissance was primarily a literary and intellectual movement centered in the 1920s and early 1930s. In general it was bounded on one side by World War I and the race riots of that period and on the other side by the stock market crash of 1929. However, it does not have such precise chronological limits.

The Harlem Renaissance was a psychology — a state of mind or an attitude shared by a number of black writers and intellectuals who centered their activities around the Harlem of the period. These men and women shared little but the consciousness that they were participants in a new awakening of black culture in the United States. They shared no common bond of political experience, background, or literary philosophy. Nevertheless, they held in common a sense of community, a feeling that all of them were part of the same endeavor.[8]

Alain Locke gave the movement a profound interpretation. Following in the scholarly footsteps of DuBois, he was a graduate of

Harvard and Oxford. A Rhodes scholar at Oxford in 1907, he studied philosophy, Greek, and modern literature at the University of Berlin and the College de France in Paris. He was devoted to the study of German culture and philosophy. Upon joining the faculty of Howard University, he first taught English but soon turned to teaching philosophy. Although he desired to teach concerning race, and especially the interaction of races affected by the African diaspora, university trustees prevented him from teaching this subject matter at this mecca of black higher education. He had not published much, and his fine education and intellectual gifts were not fully used until he found the Harlem Renaissance. Locke pursued his research and reflection with a passion. The result was a landmark volume titled *The New Negro*. His contributors amounted to a Who's Who among black American artists, intellectuals, and scholars.[9]

Locke introduces his collection with his own optimistic, powerful essay. Focusing upon the self-expression and self-determination of "the new Negro," he boldly asserted that in the very process of being transplanted, the Negro was becoming transformed.[10] Harlem had become the largest Negro community in the world. It also had become Pan-African, bringing together Negro Americans North and South, according to Locke. Blacks from city, town, and village were living together. Peasant, student, businessperson, professional, artist, poet, musician, and social outcast were all present. Each person or group had come with individual motives, but finding each other was the greatest experience. He observes, "In Harlem, Negro life is seizing upon its first chances for group expression and self-determination. It is — or promises at least to be — a race capital."[11]

He summed up his expectations of the Harlem Renaissance:

> The great social giant in this is the releasing of our talented group from the arid fields of controversy and debate to the productive fields of creative expression.... But whatever the general effect, the present generation will have added the motives of self-expression and spiritual development to the old and unfinished task making material headway and progress.[12]

The Harlem Renaissance was a brief but powerful period of black consciousness in artistic and literary modes of expression. Some of the participants in the movement were greatly prized in intellectual and cultural circles during the black power/consciousness movement of the late 1960s. I witnessed the acclaim that Sterling Brown received during the latter period at Howard University.

Civil Rights and Nonviolence

Though the civil rights movement came to its zenith in the 1960s, it had its beginning in 1954, marked by the National Association for the Advancement of Colored People (NAACP) winning the Supreme Court Decision *Brown* vs. *The Board of Education.* This decision ended the "separate but equal" legal doctrine of 1896 when the *Plessy* vs. *Ferguson* decision was rendered. Even though the 1954 court decision was hampered in implementation, it gave a powerful psychological thrust to the black struggle.

The civil rights movement was mainly integrationist, but it gave black people accomplishments they had not seen in decades. At the same time that it fostered executive orders and legislation to overcome negative blocks to progress, it built a mass movement that mobilized and politically educated millions of black people. This movement motivated a demand for human rights and black power.

Major groups such as the Student Nonviolent Coordinating Committee (SNCC), the Congress of Racial Equality (CORE), and the Southern Christian Leadership Conference (SCLC) led civil rights. We must also list Opportunities Industrialization Centers (OICs) led by Leon Sullivan. Major personalities who accomplished change included Fannie Lou Hamer, Bob Moses, Ella Baker, and Martin Luther King Jr.

Producing several fruitful results, the civil rights movement increased the liberalization of the United States system, exposed the contradictions of the American dream in the eyes of U.S. society and the world, mobilized and politically educated people who were previously outside the political process, laid the organizational and political-educational basis for continued struggle in all areas of human rights, and laid the foundation for its nationalist alternative. It opened the way for the black power movement to erupt.[13]

In chronology and spirit Martin Luther King Jr. led a movement that gave moral and spiritual undergirding to the civil rights movement. Rosa Parks, who decided not to give her bus seat to whites, initiated the Montgomery bus boycott in 1956. This boycott happened in concert with sit-ins, freedom rides, and other acts of black liberation during the same period.

King, as minister, theologian, and activist, brought a different dimension to his leadership role. He tapped into moral and spiritual resources, insisting that "morality cannot be legislated, but it can be regulated." His resources for social change came from a careful examination of the message of Jesus (love ethic) and the method of Gandhi (*satyagraha* or "truth force"). As a Baptist minister he was able to win the support of the black churches, especially in the South. Through SCLC, King was also able to gain nationwide support. His use of nonviolence as a means for social transformation moved the conscience of Americans and persons of goodwill throughout the world. His Nobel Peace Prize symbolized the global outreach of his ministry of action. He left a powerful legacy of solidarity and compassion that still lingers with us, especially in circles of Christian activism.[14]

Black Nationalism

Black Nationalism is a comprehensive concept that provides an umbrella for discussing not only the historic movement by that name but also the black power movement and Africentrism. Maulana Ron-Karenga describes this movement:

> The thrust for self-determination, self-respect and self-defense . . . gave the Black Power Movement a new vitality and dynamics. It was this thrust which to solve the Crusian-posed crisis of the Black intellectual, raised the political and cultural consciousness of the Black masses, linked our struggle with African and other Third World people and introduced the concept and practice or armed struggle in urban centers among other things.[15]

According to Karenga, Elijah Muhammad's Nation of Islam and Albert Cleage's Christian Nationalism represented the religious thrust.[16] The cultural aspect was mainly Karenga's own creation. Kawaida's ideology and the organization US represent this aspect. The most popular manifestation of Karenga's program is *Kwanzaa*. Finally, the political thrust is represented by Malcolm X, who served as an ideological and personal model for any number of nationalist groups.[17]

Based upon solid historical evidence, black nationalism that culminates in black power and consciousness in the late 1960s has a long history. Gayraud S. Wilmore has presented this well in his classic study.[18] Black nationalism, an ideology or spirit, exists wherever blacks seek to secure space to fight their own battle for freedom, in the language of Malcolm, "by any mean necessary." It is present whenever blacks enter into self-definition and become subjects of history rather than objects of history. Our ideological trail now connects with Africentrism, which is the subject of this study.

Conclusion

This chapter provides the recent historical context for understanding Africentrism. Without this excursion into the cultural history of African Americans, we are not able to appropriate the present Africentric outlook. We have traced in this setting the ideological moments in more recent black history. However, this is anchored in the late eighteenth- and nineteenth-century black experience in a Pan-African perspective. This approach is needed since Africentrism is both historical and ideological in perspective.

In our next chapter, Africentrism is examined in its deconstructive and constructive aspects as we are in search of a useable past. Although this chapter is limited to the more recent ideological shifts that have been dovetailed into Africentrism, the roots are more ancient. The recent discussions on the subject, pro and con, belong in our next chapter, a critical evaluation of Africentrism, its prospects in theological reflection, and its usefulness for ministry in black churches.

Notes

1. James W. McClendon Jr., *Biography as Theology* (Philadelphia: Trinity, 1990), introduction, v–xv.

2. W. E. B. DuBois, *Crisis* (November 1933), 247.

3. DuBois, *The World and Africa* (New York: International Publishers, 1992), 236–60. Cf. Ronald W. Walters, *Pan-Africanism in the African Diaspora* (Detroit: Wayne State University Press, 1993), 318–53.

4. P. Olisanwuche Esedebe, *Pan-Africanism: The Idea and Movement 1776–1963* (Washington, D.C.: Howard University Press, 1982), 1–2.

5. Ibid., 3.

6. Aimé Césaire, *Cahier D'un retour au pays natal* (Return to my native land), trans. Emile Snyder (Paris: Presence Africaine, 1956), 101–4.

7. Edward A. Jones, *Voices of Négritude* (Valley Forge, Pa.: Judson, 1971), 177.

8. Ibid., 199.

9. Cary D. Wintz, *Black Culture and the Harlem Renaissance* (Houston: Rice University Press, 1988), 1–2.

10. Alain Locke, *The New Negro* (New York: Atheneum, 1992), xi–xii.

11. Ibid., 6.

12. Ibid., 7.

13. Maulana Ron-Karenga, *Introduction to Black Studies*, 2nd ed. (Los Angeles: University of San-Kore Press, 1993), 165–71.

14. As a theologian and minister, I have been greatly influenced by King's ethics. The theme of reconciliation in my program of black theology comes forward directly from King's powerful witness in the area of racial understanding. See my *Liberation and Reconciliation: A Black Theology* (Philadelphia: Westminster, 1971).

15. Karenga, 173–74.

16. Ibid., 172–73.

17. Ibid., 175–79.

18. See Gayraud S. Wilmore, *Black Religion and Black Radicalism*, 3rd ed. (Maryknoll, N.Y.: Orbis, 1998), chap. 6.

Chapter 3

Evaluating Africentrism

W E TURN NOW to consider the validity of the historical claims of Africentrism. The fundamental assumption of Africentrism is that a useable past has been omitted in Western scholarship. Scholars of Africentrism assume the task of discovering and reclaiming that past. A brief account of a few of the components of this heated discussion is essential for my appraisal.

Two aspects of the claims of Africentrism are under serious attack. The most important is an assault upon classical African history in Egypt, Ethiopia, and Nubia. This Eurocentric outlook not only questions the history of Africentric scholarship but also includes the mode of thought and the cultural values of Africentrism.

This evaluation of Africentrism will begin by reflecting upon epistemology, myth, and history. *Epistemology,* or theory of knowledge, is based upon presuppositions shaped by our culture and socialization in our social environment. We are not in a position to know everything or see things from outside our range of vision. The Eurocentric outlook, based primarily upon the experience of Euro-American thought development, is limited. We learn much from getting out of our comfortable space into the experience of people with other ways of viewing things. For instance, Chinese logic differs from Aristotelian logic by allowing for a "both/and" position over against an "either/or" position. In this outlook, African American scholars have strong reasons to seek to understand how Africans have been thinking from earliest times to the present. I understand this to be what Africentrism is all about.

On Myth versus History

Myth, at least in Third World cultures, is not identical with what is untrue. Myths contain profound truth, especially in the study of morality and religion. Myths are abundant in all cultures, especially in more oral traditions, such as the African tradition. In ancient Greece, India, China, and Africa, truths are inherent in myth before they are articulated or interpreted by historians and philosophers. The study of myths has a legitimate place in all religions and cultures, and one who engages in interdisciplinary (or a phenomenological) study of human cultures will learn much from the study of myths. Joseph Campbell has spent decades studying truths found in myths around the world. The easy dismissal of myths as mere fiction is a limited point of view.

Since the strongest attack against Africentrism is based upon the nature and understanding of history, this matter deserves special attention. When we study history, we are not dealing with facts in an objective, scientific sense. The study of history is never purely objective but is also subjective. We are dealing with events or happenings that are interpreted. History involves more than language skills and textual analysis. Historical study is serious about data, but historians, each of whom has a distinct point of view, always interpret this data. The point of view of the historical is existential and cultural. That is to say, each historian has a perspective related to mentoring and nurture as well as to time and place.

Arnold Toynbee's *Study of History* and Hegel's *Philosophy of History* are particularly good examples of biased points of view. Hegel's stature in Western interpretations of history is profound, but if we took Hegel as our guide, Africentric reflections on history would be dismissed as fantasy. For him, Africa was without a civilization. It had no culture or history to consider. His conclusion obviously has more to do with his mindset than with the real Africa.

History, therefore, is more than fact; it is also the interpretation of fact. The point of view of the historian has much to do with the meaning of history to those who study it. Consequently, if those who studied history had been fair in the study of African history, African and African American ethnohistorians would have less work. Due to that negative attitude toward Africa as the Dark Continent without culture or history, black and African scholars must bring this field of knowledge up to date.

For at least five centuries, both on the continent and in the African diaspora, African history has been either neglected or interpreted in a manner to justify Western domination of African peoples. The time has come to deconstruct this Western colonialist and racist bias. The task of reclaiming our history must be done with serious and cautious scholarship. All conclusions must be based upon worthy evidence and dependable sources. Fortunately, Asante and Cheikh Anta Diop, among others, aid us in this venture.

In this endeavor, the influences of Egypt on the rest of Africa and of the rest of Africa on Egypt are important concerns. If all the influence upon advanced civilization came from Greece, why have Western scholars been so anxious to "whiten" Egyptians and take Egypt out of Africa? If we are so concerned about the political motivation behind Africentrism, why not give equal attention to the way Western history in reference to Egypt has been politicized? Any argument with force should move in both directions. My concern is not merely negative against omissions of Western historians. It is much more concerned about setting the record straight and reclaiming the heritage that belongs to Africans and African Americans for their benefit.

Quest for a Useable Past

Africentrism gets behind our preslavery past in the Africa south of the Sahara into the Africa that goes back to at least 10,000 B.C. We are now claiming as part of our roots the Africa of antiquity in the Nile Valley.

This Africentric outlook is a great challenge to Western scholarship and the worldview of peoples who come from Europe. Greco-Roman civilization laid claim to the most advanced civilization of humankind. It also assumed the leadership in most aspects of human knowledge and achievement. If Africentrists are able to substantiate their claims, much that has been taken for granted will be called into question and disestablished. Against this background, one understands why Africentrist claims are under fire.

Africentrism under Fire

Africentrists and their opponents, Eurocentrists, are engaged in a lively and extensive debate. To my knowledge Mary Lefkowitz's *Not Out of Africa: How Afrocentrism Became an Excuse to Teach Myth as History* is the most severe criticism of Africentrism in print.[1] Thus a dialogue between Asante and Lefkowitz can serve to explore the ideas of the two ends of the spectrum in this debate.[2] (Refer to chapter 2 for an in-depth discussion of Asante's Africentric position.)

Lefkowitz attacks Africentrism on historical grounds. According to Lefkowitz, Africentrists often use or misuse history to make a political point. Africentrists hold, according to this author, the view that ancient Egypt was a black African civilization. In objection, she maintains that neither the Egyptians nor the Greeks were conscious of race in the same manner as are modern societies. Ancient Egypt was a mixed society. Physical anthropology, through visual representation, suggests that Egyptians were darker than the Greeks but lighter than Nubians and other peoples living to the south of Egypt. Lefkowitz argues that Africentrists wrongly assert that Cleopatra was black. On the contrary, she claims that Cleopatra was Greek since the Ptolemies preferred Greek wives and mistresses.

Lefkowitz's strong argument against the view that Egyptians were black and a part of Africa is an attack upon the witness of Herodotus, a Greek historian who visited Egypt some time before 430 B.C. He described his visit in the second book of his *Histories*. Impressed with the antiquity of the Egyptian civilization, this Greek author refers to the similarity between what he observed in Egypt and developments in Greek culture. Greek culture postdated the ancient Egyptian civilization, according to Herodotus, and he goes on to suggest that names of the Greek gods came from Egypt and that the cult of Dionysius in Greece was inspired by the cult of Isis in Egypt.

Lefkowitz does not consider the views of Herodotus to be solid history because he uses phrases such as "roughly speaking," indicating conjecture. In other words, his ideas about Egyptian influence upon Greece were "speculative." He got a lot wrong, according to Lefkowitz, since he asserted that the Egyptians believed in the transmigration of souls, which they did not. She concludes that Herodotus presents his own admiration for the Egyptians. Although it is true that there is a shortage of definitive sources and that the reliability of some evidence is questionable, most classicists treat the works of Herodotus with respect.[3]

Lefkowitz's most decisive attack on Africentrism is less effective than she intends. The heart of the Africentric approach does not center on the African origin of civilization or the color of Cleopatra or Socrates. Africentrists insist on a proper recognition of African civilization in ancient times. Egypt is reclaimed for Africa. This appropriation means that classical Africa is a part of African roots for African Americans.

In view of the assault upon Africentrism, I consider the task of evaluation to be bifocal, a deconstructive task and a constructive task. Western scholarship has been biased against all things African. There is an almost pathological attack against the so-called Dark Continent. In view of the intellectual assault against African history, it is not surprising that black scholars are fighting back. Certainly we need to separate the wheat from the tares, but we have now moved beyond a mere popular approach to the subject at hand into the arena of serious scholarship.

The concern of Africentrists is profound; it has a history. One needs to see the problems and issues raised by Africentric scholars against the backdrop of the history of racist oppression and the improper attitude presented in classic scholarship that some European scholars have passed on as authentic for everyone. Eurocentric scholarship is now being challenged precisely because it has claimed a universal status and yet has remained provincial.

Gayraud S. Wilmore has looked at the misinformation regarding Egypt and Ethiopia that white scholars have broadcast. While white scholars previously had emphasized the "curse of Ham" as a basis for black inferiority, by 1860 they had invented the "Hamitic hypothesis," which is well stated by Wilmore:

> White biblical scholars and Egyptologists did not return to the original Hamitic hypothesis, but now insisted that the Hamites must have been a white race, and whatever can be found in African societies that is commendable must be traced to the invasion of the 'white Hamites' who ascended the Nile valley from Europe and Asia Minor to begin the process of civilization in black Africa.[4]

Add to this the development of racism in the modern West and the manner in which history, among other disciplines, has been used to substantiate racist claims, and one begins to see the comprehensive nature of the problems to be addressed. These profound issues are related to the whole history of colonialism, slavery, and racism. Black scholars must not allow the paternalism of Western scholarship to prevent them from making a serious attempt to set the record straight. Major disciplines like classics, philosophy, and anthropology are not out of the reach of competent black scholars. Black scholars, many based at Howard University, have been dealing with these concerns for decades. These scholars often studied at the best universities in Europe and the United States. In addition they also engaged in serious language and geographical studies in Africa.

As a religious philosopher I have researched ancient Greek thought for two published documents.[5] My interest in Egypt and Ethiopia was an afterthought, since I was viewing Africa from a Eurocentric perspective. As a black theologian I am now challenged to take a second look from an Africentric perspective. I shall no longer allow Euro-American scholars to be my guide.[6] I prefer to draw my own conclusions from the evidence.

The Deconstructive Task

In the interest of deconstructing the usual way of viewing the subject matter, I will set forth several critical observations.

(1) Inclusive knowledge of the ancient world is limited. Evidence is available for Africentric claims and for opposing views.

(2) Perspectives differ: No knowledge is value-free. Even physicists differ on whether the building blocks of natural phenomena are atoms or energy or both. Historians also see events from different angles of vision. In this time of the sociology of knowledge, it is doubtful that one can be a dogmatic historian. Contexts are important for what we learn from the same data. For instance, no theology of the black experience would be possible if some people did not have the courage to break with tradition. Thirty years ago, there was only white theology, which declared its universality.

(3) Careful and rigorous examination of evidence in these matters is essential. African American scholars have had to study Western sources carefully. Eurocentric scholars need to look at history from outside their own cocoon. Basil Davidson in *The African Past*, for example, has adopted this approach. Only by stepping into a different space will Eurocentric scholars be able to appreciate the Africentric perspective on historical events and facts. My own outlook has been greatly enhanced by studies and travel in the Third World. However, Eurocentric scholarship remains a part of who I am. Asante reveals competence in Eurocentric scholarship, but he challenges us to move beyond Eurocentric dogma.

I observe the same attitude in Eurocentric scholarship today that I faced in the late 1960s, even among my Howard University colleagues, black scholars, when I questioned the hegemony of Western religious thought. They regarded Eurocentric scholars as having the final word on all subjects. Now I observe the same intellectual triumphalism in the charge that Africentrism advocates a false view of history as myth. My approach is critical and cautious but open to dialogue.

(4) There are several bold experiments underway among historians as well as among philosophers and theologians. I do not see the same concerns regarding critical theory or postmodernism as I see vis-à-vis Africentrism. Could a form of intellectual paternalism be at work? Why can't African American thinkers blaze new trails in ideas, especially when the potential for wholeness and healing is so great for persons and communities? There is no reason we need to wait for the approval of the white academic establishment to do our own investigation.

In my judgment, the leading Africentric exponents have been responsible in the study and interpretation of their sources. Although some writers on the subject have not been able to give due account of their claims, they are not the pacesetters. Most scholarship is on a high level and is worthy of critical evaluation and comparative study. Dialogue, rather than condemnation, is the proper response to the exponents of Africentrism and to their opponents.[7]

A telling critique of any idea or movement must decisively question the strongest principle of its philosophy or set of beliefs. It is not sufficient to deal with the surface aspects of the weakest components of the movement in question. Many criticisms of Africentrism thus far have not examined the center or essence of Africentric claims. The essential claims of Africentrism must be taken seriously.[8]

(5) Some observers are concerned that the popular manifestation of the concept of Africentrism is ahead of the in-depth knowledge and understanding of the idea. This is one important reason for the present study.

Ideas do have consequences. This is especially the case when ideas have the possibility of personal and social transformation. Ideas are sometimes timely. It appears that Africentrism is an idea whose time has come. No serious advocate of Africentrism would see this movement as arising *de novo*. It has antecedents in the long struggle for equality and freedom for Africans and African Americans. Martin Luther King Jr. saw his mission as in tune with the *Zeitgeist,* or the spirit of the time. He observed that the freedom movement in Africa resembled the civil rights movement in the United States. In like manner, it seems that Africentrism has been affirmed widely in African American communities in view of the climate created by historic and social circumstances. The crises of identity, confusion of values, social and economic conditions, resurgence of racism, the scourge of AIDS and drugs, violence among youth, and teenage pregnancies, among many other factors, have presented a challenge to our people.

(6) Africentrism has the potential for both mass appeal and intellectual confirmation. Africentrism has thus far been a major force in the secular section of black society. Except for Cain Hope Felder, the intellectual pacesetters have been academics other than religious scholars. In fact, consultations on the subject by black scholars have been focused upon nonreligious disciplines. At first this was also true of black power, but any movement that has a powerful effect in the black community will eventually enter the black church. This is already the case in Philadelphia, where both Asante and I have taught. Philadelphia is important for the black church, which had its formal beginnings there under Richard Allen. Philadelphia exhibits a strong black presence in all aspects of life, and its black church tradition remains extremely strong and viable. Asante is in open dialogue with black pastors and laity. All seminaries in Philadelphia, in concert with the Black Clergy, Inc., are committed to ensuring that an Africentric perspective is presented in theological education. Thus, a serious theological appraisal is imperative, as indicated by the attention given to what is happening in religious circles in Philadelphia.

(7) The African American community needs unification. Africentrism has already involved black educators — including teachers at all levels — in urban centers across the nation. Advocates of Africentrism, among them Asa Hilliard, professor of education at Georgia State University, have regularly led educational tours into North Africa, especially Egypt. Asante is a consultant for several urban school districts. Workshops are held to prepare teachers to present the Africentric perspective in the education of youth. Many of these educators are leaders in the educational work in black churches,

especially in Sunday school and in youth programs. The ties between the black church, family, and school are so close that the educational and religious aspects of Africentrism easily merge.[9]

Unity between haves and have-nots may be one important result of the Africentric perspective on life. An increasing number of blacks who have made good in business and corporate sectors of life are returning to the black church as active participants in its witness. They live in the suburbs and enjoy all the material benefits of affluent citizens, but they still find that they are not fully accepted as equals. They are returning to the black churches for fellowship and spiritual nurture. Perhaps many of these people never accepted their blackness, and if that is the case, they are able to plug into the Africentric perspectives with their less fortunate brothers and sisters.

In this time of diversity, we need to be clear concerning who we are. After more than four hundred years in the West, all African Americans are "mixed." This fact, however, does not keep us from sharing the plight of the darkest-skinned persons in our midst. We need to know who we are. Our total heritage (our ancient past) is important for a positive life view and worldview. Self-affirmation is essential in our multicultural setting. The final chapter focuses on this reality, but we must suggest nevertheless that our outlook vis-à-vis other ethnics should be inclusive rather than exclusive. That is to say, a positive affirmation of our total heritage in no way requires a negative outlook on the heritage of others.

We will need to get together internally, with our brothers and sisters, as a basis for external dialogue outside the African American community. We need to know the values that are part of our heritage in order to enter into any meaningful exchanges with others. A positive affirmation of our personhood and peoplehood is a precondition for meaningful dialogue with other peoples and cultures.[10]

A Constructive Theological Appraisal

As I approach a constructive appraisal of Africentrism, I will first sum up the main concerns of those who oppose the Africentric outlook of Asante and other colleagues. The criticisms have appeared in newspapers, magazines, articles, essays, and books. Some of these writings make telling points that are not to be taken lightly. These critical efforts reflect several things. They indicate an unwillingness to consider the value of the movement. They see it as based upon fiction rather than fact. They concede its psychological and/or symbolic importance for African Americans, but they see it as bogus scholarship and a hindrance to the proper education of black youth, especially college students. They see it as a threat to multiculturalism and to democracy itself.

Obviously, I am not alarmed or surprised by these concerns of Western scholars. As a theologian of the black religious experience, I have lived for decades with these same types of challenges. It is therefore possible for me to make a more affirmative appraisal of the Africentric perspective.

I am attracted to the quest for a useable past for several reasons. First, it is significant for African Americans to claim a history that predates their enslavement. The Nile Valley civilization was highly advanced at least ten thousand years before Christ. Our belief that this civilization is part of our ancient history means a lot to our sense of "somebodiness" as individuals and as a people. Evidence of this heritage, historically speaking, is powerful, if not conclusive. It is based upon more than the wish to believe. If one takes seriously the Africentric scholarship, this is something that has to be disproved as well as amplified.

This point of view is important. Black people are more than ex-slaves. Black people were somebody before coming to these shores by the Middle Passage. We already know that we did not come here on the Mayflower. But African Americans possess a greater sense of dignity in knowing that Egypt is a part of Africa, our ancestral home, and that we can claim this noble heritage. In a state of constant and continual oppression based upon race, it is good news to lay claim to our ancient and noble heritage. This knowledge provides psychological, sociological, ethical, and spiritual benefits for African Americans. It is not surprising that both the black intellectuals and the black masses are affirming the Africentric perspective. This outlook has great potential for enriching and empowering the black church in its witness to black people. It is timely that those victimized by so much bad news should have some good news regarding who they are and who they may become.

Second, the Africentric idea provides a new approach to theology by way of thinking and reflecting upon the meaning of the Christian faith claim. If the claiming of our ancient history extends our African roots and provides a sense of dignity to black people, this new way of thinking does something more. It will provide us the freedom to create new categories of thought and language to express our faith. It will not only free us to think in an Africentric manner; it will also provide more relevant artistic ways to enrich our worship of the divine. Our thinking and our worship will no longer languish in Eurocentric cultural captivity. We will be able to affirm and celebrate in meaningful ways our unique cultural heritage. Art and music will be important means to express our faith out of the Africentric perspective and experience. Family life can be enriched and empowered by Africentric thinking. We will not necessarily reject other ways of thinking, but our center will be our cultural location, as Asante puts it. Our perspective will be expanded, and most of all, we will take pride in our heritage and ourselves. We will affirm and celebrate who we are.

Finally, there is a most attractive possibility of doing theology from the Africentric perspective. Africentrism provides a new paradigm of the Exile. Black theologians, like Latin American liberation theologians, have developed their programs using the Exodus as a principal paradigm. Womanist theologians such as Delores Williams and Diana L. Hayes have made significant use of Hagar as paradigm. But we are also a people in a strange land, in exile from the place of our ancestry. Africentrism assures us that we have that home, not merely in sub-Saharan Africa but also in the Africa of antiquity.

This exilic theology for the African American believer can only be mentioned here. However, the groundwork for this powerful redemptive theology is clearly before us. It is a place where our experience and the biblical record meet. The Exile experience is as real to us as the Exodus experience. Black theology has run with the Exodus paradigm and presented through it a powerful message of redemption. There is a real possibility of a theology of the Exile being developed from the Africentric perspective. This exilic theology has a basis not only in the biblical record but also in African American history. "Singing the Lord's song in a strange land" bears a powerful message in the minds and souls of black folk. Thus, I would suggest that the development of the theology of our experience might have several paradigms.

Womanism and Africentrism

The emergence of womanist theology has presented a challenge to black male theologians and church leaders. Since more than half of black churchgoers are women and an even larger number of these women are heading households, this movement is one that must be taken with all seriousness. The voices of black female religious scholars have only recently been sounded, and they will be around from now on. The womanist critique of the sexist attitudes and practices of black males is most telling. Womanist theologians have also extended the concerns of liberation thought to include freedom from classism as well as racism. Some womanists, through their scholarship, have developed a multidimensional outlook that includes advocating homosexual lifestyles. This concern for gay and lesbian rights is the most controversial aspect of womanism in theological circles. However, it does place on the table an issue that black male theologians and pastors must now face.

I hope that womanist theologians will be able to contribute to the well-being of all persons — male and female, young and old. Although the concern for sexual preference must be addressed, we also need to be concerned about wholesome heterosexual relationships and helping boys and girls become men and women. It will be unfortunate if black womanist theologians do not address family life concerns, since so many black women are rearing the next generation without male companionship or financial support. The plight of the black family is an urgent common ground for dialogue between black male and female theologians. Our future as a people hangs in the balance.

Black womanist theologians publish valuable new volumes every year. Womanist thinkers are having their say in all theological disciplines, in the home, in the church, in the academy, and in society. These works are vital and must be taken into account. This chapter will only set the stage for much crucial dialogue that will continue into the future. For the uninitiated the place to begin is to read carefully the volume edited by Cheryl J. Sanders, *Living the Intersection: Womanism and Afrocentrism in Theology* (Minneapolis: Fortress, 1995). In their discussions in this work, several outstanding womanist thinkers — Cheryl Townsend Gilkes, Delores Williams, Kelly Brown Douglas, Cheryl J. Sanders, and others — offer a challenge to many male Africentric thinkers. Informed by insights from Alice Walker's *In Search of Our Mother's Garden* (New York: Harcourt Brace Jovanovich, 1983), they place womanism alongside Africentrism. They desire to have their rightful place in the Africentric movement and have clearly set forth their terms of participation.

These women note the compatibility of womanist and Africentric perspectives, but they are concerned about the apparent lack of the Africentric movement's receptivity to womanist thought. At the same time that these womanist theologians claim women's personhood and freedom, they affirm Asante's essential definition that Africentricity is the belief in the centrality of Africans in postmodern history. They are impressed by Asante's assertion that male and female scholars should work together to overcome oppression. They see similarities between the meaning and purpose of womanism and Africentricity. Considering the male track record in these matters, however, they have reasons to take a wait-and-see stance.[11]

Some Issues Raised by Womanist Theologians

Some of the issues raised by womanist theologians deserve the careful attention of African American male theologians, pastors, and laity. First, some women object to the Africentric perspective on black culture and faith. The strongest objection comes from Williams,[12] who sees the same sexist tendencies that were dominant in the earlier black power nationalist movement. Second, pastors in the black denominational churches are avowedly sexist. The majority of the members of these churches, however, are female. This African American church scandal cries out for urgent attention. Third, womanist theologians challenge the masculine bias in black theology, which in turn raises other issues.

We have looked at some critical and constructive evaluations of Africentrism. Perhaps the most challenging comments to black masculine scholars, from within and without the church, come from womanist thinkers. It will be unfortunate if the sexist attitudes of black men, especially those in the ministry, should keep black men and women in conflict. We need serious conversation. If we are to save the generations through our families and churches, we must work together. This implies dialogue, mutual respect, and a common witness.

Notes

1. The title and subtitle of Mary Lefkowitz's *Not Out of Africa: How Afrocentrism Became an Excuse to Teach Myth as History* indicates a bias against Africa and the Africentric movement. Even though the author's scholarship is impressive, it does not conceal or substantiate the author's outlook, which is solidly against any legitimate claims of Africentric scholarship.

2. George G. M. James in *Stolen Legacy: Greek Philosophy Is Stolen Egyptian Philosophy* (New York: Philosophical Library, 1954) attempts to stake a claim for the ultra-Africentric position. It was intended, according to its author, to improve race relations. In the present debate, however, it may do more harm than good. This volume has inadequate documentation, and when one attacks well-established views, one should document carefully, using the best available sources. Scholars who are specialists on the subject must be able to read behind the writers and examine sources.

3. Lefkowitz's second chapter is crucial for the presentation here. She brings in Martin Bernal's *Black Athena: The Afroasiatic Roots of Classical Civilization* (New Brunswick, N.J.: Rutgers University Press, 1987), 1: *The Fabrication of Ancient Greece, 1785–1985*, 2: *The Archaeological and Documentary Evidence* (1991). Lefkowitz is obviously impressed with Bernal's masterful study. She has put together a collection of essays in response to Bernal's challenge: Mary R. Lefkowitz and Guy MacLean Rogers, eds., *Black Athena Revisited* (Chapel Hill: University of North Carolina Press, 1996). I will not pursue this discussion further. It is related to the interests of the Afrocentrists; however, it complicates the discussion with reference to Asia as well as Africa. It does, however, question the hegemony of the Eurocentric point of view espoused by Lefkowitz and her colleagues.

I have reviewed a number of editorial essays on this discussion. Some representative reports are George F. Will, "Intellectual Segregation, or Afrocentrism's many myths constitute condescension toward African-Americans," *Newsweek* (February 19, 1996), 78; John Elson, "Attacking Afrocentrism," *Time* (February 19, 1996), 66, a brief presentation of Lefkowitz's outlook; John Beck, "Afrocentrists turn history upside down," *New Haven Register,* March 11, 1996, A6.

Gerald Early provides an excellent summary of the meaning of Afrocentrism in his "Understanding Afrocentrism" in *Civilization* (July/August 1995): 31–39.

4. Gayraud S. Wilmore, *Black Religion and Black Radicalism*, 3rd ed. (Maryknoll, N.Y.: Orbis, 1998), 47.

5. See J. Deotis Roberts, *A Philosophical Introduction to Theology* (Philadelphia: Trinity Press International, 1991) and *From Puritanism to Platonism in Seventeenth-Century England* (The Hague: Martinus Nijoff, 1968). Cf. Cornel West, *Prophesy Deliverance!* (Philadelphia: Westminster,

1982). His chapter titled "A Genealogy of Modern Racism," 47–49, is especially helpful.

6. A similar observation could be made of Albert Schweitzer. Though he spent more than fifty years as a medical missionary in Africa, his writings on the philosophy of civilization reveal that he did not come to appreciate the richness of the history and culture of Africans.

7. The attempt to enculturate Christianity in theological reflection in Asia and Africa has met the "imperialism" of Western scholarship head-on. See Justin S. Ukpong, "Enculturation in Africa: A Major Challenge," *Theology Digest* 44, no. 3 (fall 1997): 231–33. See also Peter C. Phan, "Experience and Theology: an Asian Liberation Perspective," ibid., 230.

8. It is worthy of note that several of the most severe criticisms on Afrocentrism have come from journalists and not from able scholars in classics or history.

9. Several leading scholar-pastors, for example, Jeremiah Wright Jr., Floyd Flake, and William Watley, have established educational programs in an institutional church setting.

10. Much of the scholarship in support of the Africentric perspective harks back to significant work of Cheikh Anta Diop of Senegal. Diop, an Egyptologist, studied in Paris and knew both African and European ideas and cultures well. Asante acknowledges Diop's mentorship.

11. See Delores S. Williams, *Sisters in the Wilderness* (Maryknoll, N.Y.: Orbis Books, 1994), 167–70.

12. Ibid., 185–87.

Chapter 4

Biblical Hermeneutics in Africentric Perspective

Do you have any relatives or friends who either left the church or refuse to attend church, saying that Christianity is a "White man's religion"? Have you ever heard from them the idea that the Bible was written by, for, and about White people? Do they tell you that White Christians were major participants in the slave trade, and that White people have used Christianity as an "opiate," to keep Black people docile and servile?[1]

THE BIBLE, which is a guide for Christians in personal and social relations, must be interpreted. Scriptures are often interpreted to the advantage of those who are reading the texts, but it is equally important to seek to understand how the Bible challenges us.

The December 1, 1997, telecast of Robert Schuller's *Hour of Power* demonstrated how one can interpret the Bible to further one's ideology and program. The message was on what Schuller called "Christian Capitalism," and it was based on the parable of the talents in Matthew 25. Schuller used the Scripture to support his "possibility thinking," with a strong emphasis upon investment for profit. He then used John Wesley's notable saying "Earn all you can, save all you can, and give all you can" to buttress his outlook. A necessary critique of the greed often associated with profitmaking was missing. For Wesley, who was concerned about elevating the poor, the emphasis seemed to be on giving all you can. In the United States, however, the political, economic, and theocratic views of Adam Smith and John Calvin have overshadowed Wesley's initial impulse

To his credit Schuller mentioned Jesus' saying regarding the final judgment and our Lord's praise of those who help the needy, but his reference appeared to be an afterthought. The latter observation received scant attention alongside of his picture of profitmaking as praiseworthy. The ease with which one can use a passage of Scripture to one's advantage shows the need for serious Bible study in a critical sense and not in a merely literal sense.

The Bible in the African American Church Tradition — Quest for Biblical Authority

Most black Christians are Protestant. The Bible is their primary (if not sole) source for knowledge of God and guidance for the expression of the Christian faith in personal and social life. (The Bible and tradition are, in many cases, equally important for Roman Catholics.) Therefore, the Bible must be carefully studied and understood as a basis for Christian discipleship.

The Bible as a whole is essential for our faith, but not all portions of Scripture are on the same level. The New Testament, especially the segments on the life, ministry, teaching, death, and resurrection of Jesus Christ, serve as a standard by which Christians seek to understand the entire Bible. We understand our Christian faith not only through what the Old Testament tells us as it points to Jesus but also through what has been discovered by Christian experience over the centuries.

The Bible is large and complicated, containing many documents by various authors. These materials gathered over extensive space and time were also were also subject to the work of editors. Much of the Bible was passed along by word of mouth for a long time before it was written down, and thus it is impossible to identify the original authors of all the books of the Old Testament. Even in the New Testament, the four Gospels were written from fragments and not put into their present form until forty years after Jesus' death. Paul's letters to the newly founded churches were written earlier than were the Gospels. The faith of early Christians prompted the compiling of the rest of the New Testament.

Christian scholars have done much research on various parts of the Bible. They have undertaken studies to find out, as far as possible, who wrote each book, when it was written, and the religious and social conditions under which the writing was done. Literary studies are performed to determine the accuracy of translations. Identification of the different literary forms gives us a better knowledge of the Bible than was previously possible. We are able to observe the unity of the Bible's message in spite of its various literary forms.

The Bible is a message from God through humans in history. Through its words God speaks to inspire us to deeper faith and holy living. As I have said elsewhere,

> The Bible is the Word of God, regardless of the limitations of the human words through which it comes to us. In spite of its several authors and their social setting, the Bible has a unity in its central message of God's love, mercy, and compassion for people, even in their sinfulness. Though the Bible is not to be taken *literally,* it is to be taken *seriously.* We should read it as we would an important message from a dear friend sent by a middle person. God's Word is spoken through the human words of the writers of the books of the Bible.[2]

The importance of the Bible, and its composition, and its challenge for study and meaning set high standards for biblical interpreters "rightly dividing the word of truth" (2 Timothy 2:15). "The Bible is the living Word of God in so far as it bears witness to God's revealing the divine mind and will to us in Jesus Christ. The supreme norm of the Christian faith is the Word made flesh. God comes to us savingly in Christ. We must never substitute the written words of the Bible for the Living Word. God's Word is God's saving act in Jesus Christ."[3]

That is to assert that by the agency of the Holy Spirit God takes the written word up into the living Word. The Word of God is contained in Scripture, and the Scripture is the Word of God as it bears witness to the living Word of God as revealed in Jesus Christ. We must therefore use our best knowledge and judgment to interpret Scriptures.

The interpretation of the Bible is serious in that our faith rests upon biblical inspiration and authority. In the words of a noted black preacher, Sandy Ray, "One should not get into deep water in a paper boat." Systematic and philosophical theology requires serious study of the Bible among many related disciplines. Nevertheless, this only deepens my appreciation for those who devote all their spiritual and intellectual gifts in the study of the two Testaments of the Bible, their languages, literature, and texts. At the same time, we must insist upon careful and thoughtful scholarship from those who assume this awesome responsibility. The Bible comes to us through our culture, but it also remains transcultural. Its saving relation is for all people.

A Brief Look at Black Biblical Hermeneutics

Black biblical hermeneutics that accompanies the development of black theology must be distinguished from Africentric biblical hermeneutics. Professor James Cone laid the groundwork for biblical interpretation within black theology: "Christian theology is a theology of liberation. It is a rational study of the being of God in the world in light of the existential situation of an oppressed community, relating the forces of liberation to the essence of the gospel, which is Jesus Christ."[4]

The "Exodus Paradigm" is, for Cone, the exegetical perspective for understanding God's liberating message for the oppressed. It is also a clue for understanding the Old Testament, because biblical interpretation for Cone is grounded christologically. The Exodus motif is reinforced by the Lukan text (Luke 4:18–19), which describes Jesus' sense of mission, the "liberation" of humankind. Cone writes that "if the history of Israel and the New Testament description of the historical Jesus reveal that God is a God who is identified with Israel because it is an oppressed community, the resurrection of Jesus means that all oppressed peoples become his people. Herein lies the universal note implied in the gospel message of Jesus."[5]

The black biblical scholar Robert A. Bennett uses his expertise in Old Testament study to reinforce the liberation outlook of Cone. In *God's Work of Liberation,* Bennett describes for us "a journey through the Old Testament with the liberation heroes of Israel." In his study of the Hebrew Bible, he examines the calls and missions of many great personages of Israel, the patriarchs, Moses, the judges, David, the prophets, and the wise men and women of ancient Israel. Liberation is the motif that opens up the message of the saving revelation of the Old Testament. "The liberation heroes of Israel, such as Abraham, Moses, David, Isaiah, and Job, were those folk who proclaimed to the people what God had done and was doing in their midst as savior and liberator."[6]

Since Bennett assumes the unity of the Bible and an essential continuity of the Old Testament message of liberation with God's saving revelation to all persons and peoples, his study on the Old Testament is strong support for Cone's theological perspective on liberation. Black theology appears to have inspired Bennett's significant contribution to Old Testament interpretation. As a biblical scholar, Bennett fully participated in conversations with those of us forging a theological program out of the experience of black Christians, past and present. He serves as a prime example of one who takes the theme of liberation into careful biblical study.

Latta R. Thomas, a college professor and a pastor of a black Baptist church for many years, has used his insights to interpret the Bible in these two contexts. He is concerned about theological reflection on the message of the Bible for all people, but he is especially concerned for the liberation of the oppressed. He brings evangelical and liberation motifs together.

In *Biblical Faith and the Black American,* Thomas sets forth his outlook on biblical interpretation in four basic assertions.[7] First, "The Bible is a collective document that grew out of and is about God's liberation of people from human sin and oppression." Second, "The Bible pictures the real God of heaven and earth and of Jesus Christ as always concentrating his liberating efforts and concerns where human beings are in need." Third, "Before the Bible can be seen in all its liberating purity and power, effort must be made to identify and cut through those motives, myths, and interpretations, whether deliberate or accidental, which result in the attempts to twist the Bible in support of Black enslavement and White racism." Fourth, "Black people need the liberating power and direction available in the biblical faith as never before, and should fully embrace them."[8]

In these observations, Thomas sees the Bible as an important document for use in the lives of oppressed people, a great number of whom are black. In a powerful summary statement, Thomas describes the Bible as a document of physical and spiritual liberation.

> In reality the Bible, when allowed to come through without human tampering by people with shallow minds and evil motives, not only *does not* support human oppression, but also *urges human rebellion* against mistreatment of human beings as a matter of commitment to the God of heaven, earth and history.
>
> The central theme of the New Testament is that God himself came to man's hopeless and helpless situation (the incarnation) to lift human beings from the condition characterized by human sin and misery, and through Jesus, the Christ, began his work with the farthest down — the have-nots, the enslaved, the outcasts, the wounded, and the "nobodies" of this world.[9]

Thomas, like Cone, calls witness to the Moses of the Exodus and the author of Luke in support of his outlook on biblical interpretation. Thomas's case is similar to my own input into the discussion. Elsewhere I have discussed how the West African understanding of God was similar to the biblical God, especially regarding divine creation and providence. Black slaves brought from Africa to America a view of community that emphasized individual responsibility within community, the relation between human beings, and the relation between the living and the dead. Religion embraced all of life. Therefore, in my view, it was not difficult for black slaves to understand God as one who acts redemptively in the life of a people.

> When African slaves were introduced to the Bible, they were able to derive meaning from it that was hidden to their oppressors. They understood God against the background of traditional beliefs in a Supreme God. They were aware of the power and moral integrity of God. Jehovah, as described in the Old Testament, was a close facsimile of the African Supreme being they had known. Facing a situation of great hardship, the liberation of the Hebrews from Egyptian bondage caught their fancy. As a Black oppressed people, facing daily the White oppressor, the Exodus took on a political as well as a religious meaning.[10]

We have added African roots to biblical hermeneutics and at the same time maintained the liberation motif. In concert with Latin American liberation theologians, we have called for "a hermeneutic of suspicion." Just as theology as a whole has assumed a different approach from below, biblical hermeneutics is required to make a new departure.

Liberationists share additional insights with others who deal with method in biblical interpretation. Thomas has indicated some pitfalls when we merely follow others. We need to examine the meaning of certain buzzwords such as "horizons" and "hermeneutical circle." We must keep clearly in view our real concerns. Limiting our biblical interpretation to liberation themes would be inadequate. However, we must insist that liberation from oppression be included in any adequate program of biblical interpretation. Our concern would not be centered on race issues alone, though these might well be central to our project. Another way of saying this is that we would move from the particular to the universal. For the African American biblical interpreter, oppression based on racial oppression would be a crucial starting point, for the more we understand how the Bible addresses any one form of oppression, the more we develop a solidarity with others who experience another form of oppression.

Black Culture and Biblical Hermeneutics

Black womanist scholars have much to say on this subject (see chap. 3), but two male colleagues, James H. Evans and Stephen Breck Reid, have given special attention to black literature and fine arts as they affect theology and Bible.

In *Spiritual Empowerment in Afro-American Literature* Evans discusses four "moments" of literary-cultural expression. The first religious moment is the "pure" African American autobiography. The slave narrative is its prototype, and Frederick Douglass is the example. The second moment is the "cultural act" in the form of creation, in which religion seeks to create a new order for the community. Rebellion is superseded by a religious affirmation turned inward. Christian history is reinterpreted, and Christian doctrine is rewritten from the perspective of the oppressed. This perspective is represented by what Evans calls "fictive" autobiography, in which to some extent the written word hides the self for the sake of the group. A new worldview is forged.[11] Booker T. Washington's *Up from Slavery* illustrates this second moment.

The third moment takes the form of a dialectical struggle. Its goal is the recovery of the self in the creative process, and its chief means is critical-reflexive self-examination. Here religious expression "seeks a balance that includes the inner harmony of personal authentication and outer peace with the social environment."[12] Evans uses W. E. B. DuBois's comments on "a double consciousness."

Finally, a fourth moment takes the form of cultural renewal through the recovery of origins. The goal is to counter the effects of temporal and spatial dislocation. Theologically, eschatology becomes a primary theme. That is, one seeks to discern the role and authority of the past and the anticipated future in the present struggle for liberation.[13] An example of this fourth moment is depicted by Toni Morrison's *Song of Solomon.*

Evans illustrates these four cultural moments in black religious literary expression as they express and define the struggle for liberation. He evaluates the writings of Frederick Douglass, Booker T. Washington, Richard Wright, and Toni Morrison to illustrate the four moments of black religious and cultural expression.

Though Evans is writing mainly as a theologian, his perspective is valuable for black biblical scholars. To understand the mindset of black believers is to enter into their use of Scripture and its meaning. His insights take us beyond the more rational approach of most black male theologians and enter the world of several women who have a strong literary background and interests. He also takes culture more seriously than some black male theologians have. Thus he opens the way to a more fruitful encounter with Africentrism:

> The faith of Afro-Americans involves the risk of believing and acting on that belief — that God is on the side of the oppressed in history. The Afro-American risks believing that the experiences and the vision of Afro-Americans can be accurately captured within literate modalities and profitably shared even with those who do not directly share those experiences.[14]

Stephen Breck Reid, a biblical theologian, helps us observe how a deep encounter with culture enhances our understanding of the Bible. Reid observes: "Black biblical hermeneutics, like those of any oppressed people, is ultimately the quest for identity as God's believing community. This entails the interpretation of Black experience, which calls for the interpretation of other data, as well as scripture. A Black biblical hermeneutic must interpret both Black experience and biblical text."[15]

According to Reid, the question of identity organizes black biblical interpretation. Since the black church in the United States began as a slave church, black biblical hermeneutics must reach back to the antiquity of oppression. Reid observes: "Any Black biblical hermeneutic must be tested by the blood of antiquity. The blood of Black Christians in North Africa and Ethiopia and the blood of Black Christians shed in the red clay of Georgia and Alabama are the litmus tests of any Black biblical theology."[16]

The task of the black biblical scholar is to discover anew the tradition of Scripture in the black church and culture and to bring this black church tradition together with Scripture. The scholar "holds Black culture in one hand and the Bible in the other."[17] There is to follow a critical reading of the text, the recovery of the black interpretation of the text, and the application of the text to the life experience of the black community.[18] Reid draws upon nonbiblical material, such as poetry, music, novels, and plays. The spiritual "Dry Bones" interprets Ezekiel 37 and offers a good example of how aspects of black culture enhance the meaning of biblical text.

While much of black biblical thought comes from the Hebrew Bible, Reid reminds us that the Christ event is crucial. He lifts up two Christology traditions in the black church. The imitation of Christ tradition raises the question about how we are to conform our lives to the example of Christ. The victorious Christ tradition raises the question about the political effects of the reign of God.[19] Reid's treatise opens the door for the cultural emphasis in Africentrism to be a means to biblical interpretation. As an Old Testament scholar, he values biblical theology and the centrality of Christology in understanding the Bible.

The Significance of the Africentric Biblical Hermeneutic

I have attempted to lay a secure foundation for our discussion on Africentric biblical hermeneutics. For me, this is critical for our Christian faith. First, it is essential that one struggle with the meaning of Africentrism, which is more than some popular versions of biblical interpretation imply. Second, the black or African presence in the Bible is not the essence of Africentric hermeneutics. This can be a merely cultural/historical fact—it may not have much to do with the saving message of Scripture. Thus, I have been selective in presenting the representative persons involved in this awesome task. They have the scholarly credentials, but they also exemplify an appreciation for the Bible as an authoritative faith document. They affirm that the Bible contains God's message of salvation for a sinful humanity.

In what way then can we embrace a genuine Africentric approach to the Bible? How may we do this and yet retain the Bible as an authentic book of God's salvific revelation? In order to answer these questions concerning the Bible, we will need to be clear regarding our theological appraisal of the notion of Africentricity. Africentricity embraces much of black theology and biblical interpretations based upon the meaning of blackness as applied to religious experience.

From a historical perspective, Africentricity goes back to the beginnings of African history based in Egypt and Ethiopia rather than in the early West African kingdoms. This history includes the latter histories but antedates them. For instance, Africentricity reclaims Egypt for Africa. It rejects the claim of those historians and classicists who place Egypt elsewhere and who hold that Greco-Roman civilization is the norm.

Africentricity sees Egypt, the initiator of civilization as known in the West, at the fountainhead of Western civilization. At the same time, Africentricity insists that Egypt belongs to black Africa. The Egypt that displayed an advanced civilization thousands of years in the era before Christ and that antedates Judaic and Greco-Roman civilizations is part of the history of black Africa.

Since African American ancestry is classical Africa, we had a noble history before our enslavement. We can look behind slavery and no longer define our history or our peoplehood by what happened in or through slavery. Our recognition of our ancient history helps us improve our sense of self-worth and our "somebodiness" as a people.

When we bring this Africentric perspective into biblical hermeneutics, it has profound meaning. The discoveries in the Bible of persons and places that hark back to Egypt or Ethiopia in the period before Christ become important to our life of faith. These discoveries affirming our kinship with ancient and noble people in classical Africa enrich and empower us. Thus Africentrism can enhance our cultural roots and empower our life of faith at the same time.

Cain Hope Felder's Project

In lifting up Cain Hope Felder's contribution to biblical scholarship, I affirm the role of many other African American scholars. Clarice Martin, Renita Weems, Thomas Hoyt, Randell Bailey, Vincent L. Wimbush, and Charles Copher are among those worthy of note. However, we can best highlight the Africentrist movement by examining the contribution of one person, and Felder is a good example. His leadership has been well received by his colleagues and is evident in *Stony the Road We Trod*, a volume of black biblical scholarship that he edited.[20]

Felder's perspective on biblical interpretation began in his skepticism of Western appropriations of the biblical message. This led him to develop a course titled "Ethiopia and Arabia in Biblical Antiquity" at Princeton Theological Seminary in 1980. This course, according to Felder, led to "confession and a new beginning."[21] He recalls,

> I began to realize that my own theological training and graduate studies had treated most of ancient Africa as peripheral or insignificant. I also recognized that aspects of European historiography and archeology have been tainted by a self-serving, racialist hermeneutic that sought not objective truth but careful, "scientific" ways of reinforcing the superiority and normative character of Western culture...as the *sole arbitrator* of the biblical tradition.[22]

This new awareness led him to confront the "distortions of the sacred story." After careful research and analysis, he concluded that his new project required several ingredients: "(1) an intentional 'African' identity; (2) a new skepticism about prevailing Eurocentric exegesis, hermeneutics, and historiography; and (3) a renewed commitment to the New Testament vision of liberation as a self-perpetuating process."[23]

Felder then called upon his unusual background and talents to constructively interpret the Bible with the black religious and church tradition in view. He had studied African American and African history at Howard University under some of the leaders in this historical tradition,[24] and his work in classics, languages, and philosophy also served him well. In addition, however, he entered the circle of Africentric scholars with his biblical mandate clearly in view. His work with Ephraim Isaac, an Ethiopian scholar, and his critical dialogue with Asante greatly enriched his background.

Felder's evaluation has been both critical and positive, and he has made an enormous contribution toward greater biblical understanding in the academy and the church. A comprehensive evaluation of his accomplishment is not possible here, but we can note three aspects of his biblical interpretation: his canon research, his recontextualization program, and his reflection of the black presence in the Bible.

In a paper presented to the members of the Society for the Study of Black Religion (SSBR) meeting in Chicago (October 20, 1984), Felder surprised and electrified his listeners by his "manifesto."[25] In the spirit of Karl Barth, he unfolded his version of "the strange new world of the Bible." His position against the background of deep insights into classical African history in Egypt and Ethiopia broadened the conception of African roots and closed the ranks between those of Haley's *Roots* perspective and the new Africentric outlook.

Much that he observed concerning classical Africa has been presented. However, his appropriation of this perspective for biblical interpretation is crucial.

First, he tackles "historical relativism and cultural subjectivity in canon formation." Canon formation took place over hundreds of years, and Felder is concerned about those "*who* were the persons *deciding on* which books were to be omitted."[26] He raises the issues of the worldview, political authority, and cultural or racial self-interest of the decision makers. He points to the scant attention given by Western biblical scholars to the formation of the ancient Ethiopian canon as a case in point.[27] Thus, for Felder, "a substantive critique of the process of canonization leads Blacks inescapably 'back to Africa.' "[28]

Felder suggests that more needs to be said. The formation of the New Testament canon is tied up with triumphalism in Christianity. He finds traces of this triumphalism in Colossians, Ephesians, and the Pastoral Epistles. From Constantine to Justinian, Christianity becomes the religion of the victorious parties. Such writings as the Gospel of the Egyptians or the Gospel to the Hebrews, both widely used in Egypt, failed to be accepted into the canon. Radical Christian groups, both Gnostic and Jewish Christians, become the vanquished parties without canonical portfolio. Felder's effort to link canon formation with the rise of triumphalism in Christianity is quite persuasive.[29]

The second effort in Felder's program of biblical interpretation is recontextualization. He describes recontextualization as "a process of rediscovering some essential features of the Black religious experience in Africa, including but not limited to African Traditional Religions and doing this as one enters a new dialogue of liberation and spirituality as found in the Bible."[30]

Felder summons the witness of such authorities as William Leo Hansberry and Cheikh Anta Diop to establish his perspective. He maintains that early cross-continental migrations in Africa can explain why diverse tribes of Africans have so much in common, religiously speaking.

This is exactly why diverse tribes of Africa have a ritual, belief, sacrifice and theological system that shares so many common features. Indeed, such notions as a Supreme Being/Creator/Protector God, the multiplicity of spirits (demonic and Angelic), a notion of communal solidarity and sharing, a view about the reality of the Afterlife are found respectively in the religious experience of the ancient Egyptians, African Traditional Religions and the Bible itself.[31]

The third and final observation in this study has to do with Felder's emphasis upon the presence of Africa in the Bible. In my view it is the most popular and problematic part of Felder's study, because many black leaders, clergy and lay, have seized upon this aspect of Felder's research without considering his corpus of scholarship. To be meaningful, this emphasis needs the undergirding of a broader set of issues and facts. Without these issues and facts, it is a misnomer to refer to such biblical interpretation as Africentric.

Felder illustrates his claim for significant African presence in the Bible by devoting his second chapter to "Ancient Ethiopia and the Queen of Sheba."[32] In it he demonstrates a careful interpretation of a passage in Africentric perspective, an interpretation that reflects a body of historical, cultural, literary, and biblical knowledge. In this way Felder has set high standards for all persons seeking the black presence in the Bible. While I celebrate this effort and think it may help build self-esteem, this type of interpretation should be done carefully and with integrity, in keeping with the place of the Bible in Christian worship and life.

Conclusion

In this chapter, I have discussed a number of concerns regarding the place of the Bible in the life of black Christians. After looking at biblical authority, I discussed hermeneutics and attempted to establish a continuity and a discontinuity between black biblical hermeneutics and the new Afrocentric biblical hermeneutic. The aspects of Felder's program that cast light on the subject have been presented.

I have concluded this chapter by affirming the significance of the Africentric perspective on biblical interpretation. For black Christians who are Africentric, the Bible remains a holy Book. It is the main written text for the affirmation of the Christian faith. We must celebrate this exciting breakthrough in the searching of Scriptures. Furthermore, the identification of authentic persons of color in biblical study is inspirational to black believers. A part of the theologian's task is to appraise scholarship in all theological disciplines, "rightly dividing the word of truth."

Notes

1. Jeremiah A. Wright Jr., *Africans Who Shaped Our Faith*, edited by Colleen Binchett (Chicago: The Urban Ministries, 1995), preface, 9.

2. See J. Deotis Roberts, *Christian Beliefs* (Valley Forge, Pa.: Office of Evangelism, ABC/USA, 1981), 10.

3. Ibid., 13.

4. James H. Cone, *A Black Theology of Liberation* (Maryknoll, N.Y.: Orbis, 1990), 1.

5. Ibid., 3.

6. Robert A. Bennett, *God's Work of Liberation* (Wilton, Conn.: Morehouse-Barlow, 1976), 4.

7. Latta R. Thomas, *Biblical Faith and the Black Americans* (Valley Forge, Pa.: Judson, 1976).

8. Ibid., 12.

9. Ibid.

10. See J. Deotis Roberts, *Black Theology Today* (Toronto: The Edwin Mellen Press, 1983). Cf. Duncan S. Ferguson, *Biblical Hermeneutics* (Atlanta: John Knox, 1986), chap. 5.

11. James H. Evans Jr., *Spiritual Empowerment in Afro-American Literature* (Toronto: The Edwin Mellen Press, 1987), 2.

12. Ibid., 11.

13. Ibid., 15.

14. Ibid., 20.

15. Stephen Breck Reid, *Experience and Tradition: A Primer in Black Biblical Hermeneutics* (Nashville: Abingdon, 1990), 15.

16. Ibid., 13.

17. Ibid., 16.

18. Ibid., 19.

19. Ibid., 20.

20. Cain Hope Felder, ed., *Stony the Road We Trod* (Minneapolis: Fortress, 1991).

21. Cain Hope Felder, *Troubling Biblical Waters* (Maryknoll, N.Y.: Orbis, 1989), 8.

22. Ibid., 22.

23. Ibid., 15.

24. Ibid., 10.

25. Cain Hope Felder, unpublished paper, "The Bible as Foundational for Future Meaning in the Black Religious Experience," presented to the Society for the Study of Black Religion (SSBR) meeting in Chicago, October 20, 1984. Much that he presented in the initial paper is repeated in *Troubling Biblical Waters*.

26. Ibid., 9–10. Cf. *Troubling Biblical Waters*, 14–16.

27. Felder, unpublished paper, 15.

28. Ibid.

29. Felder, *Troubling Biblical Waters*, 15.

30. Felder, unpublished paper, 12.

31. Ibid., 12–13.

32. Cf. Edward Ullendorff, *Ethiopia and the Bible*, The Schweich Lecture for 1967 (Oxford: Oxford University Press, 1968), 131–33.

Chapter 5

The Africentric Perspective and Christian Theology

I N THIS CHAPTER I assess the extent to which Africentrism is compatible with the doctrine of God that is central to the Christian faith. This evaluation is needed in a climate of uncertainty among both clergy and laity in the black church, and some of my experiences illustrate this challenge.

In the spring of 1998 I was invited to be a retreat leader for a group of black United Methodist ministers from Raleigh, North Carolina, who meet annually at Myrtle Beach, South Carolina. An impressive segment of this retreat was a dialogue with Bishop Edwards, who is white. The first day, I was mainly an observer. African American church leaders and their bishop discussed several burning issues — sexism, racism, and mixed racial appointments. Both the questions put to the bishop and the bishop's responses were significant for my lecture and discussion.

At the center of their concern was how to minister when a black minister is assigned to a congregation in which a sizable number of whites participate. In North Carolina a number of Native Americans also often take part. How does a black American pastor maintain integrity in a congregation that is both interracial and cross-cultural? In this situation one needs to be pro-black without being anti-white. In other words, I need to be inclusive in embracing Africentrism, to affirm African and African American cultural history without rejecting the cultural history of other people.

On special occasions, such as celebrations of rites of passage, one should wear African dress in order to display pride in one's roots and to share cultural aspects of one's heritage. These occasions would be opportunities to teach about the importance of this display of culture.

57

Information, programs, worship, and the like would make the Africentric outlook more meaningful to participants and observers. In this way one would be enriching the lives of blacks and others while opening up an appreciation for cultures other than one's own.

However, it is essential that we get behind the concern expressed by those at the retreat to the question raised in this segment of our study: How can Christian doctrine be enhanced by the Africentric perspective?

Theism and Africentrism

In London I led a retreat for the Simeon of Cyrene Institute. I had been asked by Canon Sihon Goodridge, now Anglican bishop in the Windward Islands, to speak on "the color of God." This engagement occurred in 1993, before I began a serious study of Africentrism. Nevertheless, my lecture and discussion with black church leaders from Africa and the West Indies, together with a few whites, anticipated some of the theological reflection in this study. This is especially true of the doctrine of God.

"What color is God?" is a serious question. If we take the question in a literal sense, it will be rightly rejected. God is Spirit, and Spirit has no color. God is universal. It is not possible to particularize God. However, if we unravel the symbolic meaning of the question, it can convey a powerful message for how we understand God and how we relate to the divine ultimate of our faith. We are persons who have individual centers of awareness, and we also develop in a social setting. God reveals Godself to us, but the particular experiences of individuals and communities of faith condition the response of faith.

Central to our discussion is the doctrine of God. Theology is *logos* of *theos*, "thinking about God." Thus, the way we understand God is central to our Christian beliefs. Christian theology, at least in the Protestant tradition, is based upon biblical revelation. The biblical assertion "In the beginning God" has great implications for our faith. The first sentence in the Bible, "In the beginning God created the heaven and the earth" (Genesis 1:1) is loaded with theological meaning. God is the author of creation. As stated in the creeds, God is Maker of heaven and the earth. Nature and supernature are grounded in God's creative act. The Bible does not devote attention to proofs for the divine existence. God's existence is grasped by faith rooted in an experience with God. This faith is eloquently described in the eleventh chapter of the book of Hebrews.

The Africentric cultural worldview places Africa at the center of our perspective. African American life and history are not defined by the experience of slavery and beyond. We are taken back to classical Africa in the era before Christ in Egypt, Ethiopia, and Cush. The Africentric perspective reclaims this ancient and noble civilization as that which belongs to us as a people. Egypt, for example, is put back into Africa. We affirm our dignity as a people without downgrading the status of any other people. We categorically reject an inferior place in the human family.

Africentrism enriches our sense of worth through our African roots. We are proud of who we are because of who we were before we became slaves. We, ourselves, must define who we are. If we allow others to define us, we will be swallowed up in the amorphous perspective known as pluralism or diversity. "*African* American" will be meaningful only if we are able to see it for ourselves. An inclusive version of Africentrism also allows others to affirm who they are.

What does it mean to say that God is black? We need to restate briefly what blackness means in the black theology movement in which I have participated. For us *blackness* has profound meaning—ontological as well as symbolic meaning. It says something about who we are. It erases and moves beyond the images of us in the white mind. Knowing and understanding our African heritage as black heritage is a means to self-definition and the identity of a people.

The discussion of blackness moves smoothly into Africentrism. Africentrism builds upon African American gains in self-definition during the black power/black consciousness era. Because Africentrism connects us with classical Africa, it provides an enhanced meaning from the cultural-historical point of view. Our African roots are deeper and richer still. With this Africentric view in mind, we must look carefully at our understanding of the Christian God.

Toward an Africentric View of God

The Christian God is revealed as a triune God who has superlative attributes of love, wisdom, and power. God not only is manifest in

Scripture but also is encountered in all of nature and history. God reveals Godself in a trinitarian manner. Each mode of God's existence has revelatory significance in creation, providence, and redemption. God's identity and character are evident in God's work in the world and through human life. The Christian encounters God as Creator, Redeemer, and Sanctifier.

God has a well-balanced ethical character: God is merciful but also just. God as the divine person meets us on the ground of ethical demand and judgment. God is a God of mercy, love, grace, and goodness. God is righteous, holy, and just. It is significant that God is at once merciful and just. God comforts and heals, but the divine one also judges and disturbs; God is lovingly just.

Our experience serves as a receptacle or channel through which God's revelation appears. Who we are and where we are determines the impact of God's revelation. This does not imply a total relativism. There is an objective and ontological dimension of God's address to us. However, it becomes meaningful only when we appropriate it in the place and condition where we stand.

The biblical question "Adam, where are you?" can be addressed to each person. God's address to us is personal, but it is also social. We are called as individuals, but we are also summoned as a people. Because of historical events, as well as human sin and evil, our *Sitz im Leben,* our situation in our living world is diverse. Among us are oppressors and victims of oppression. Whatever our condition, God calls us by name and meets us where we are.

The Triune God and Human Liberation

Karl Barth correctly included the trinitarian revelation of God in a discussion of revelation. However, in Barth's Bible-centered, christocentric view of revelation, the liberating work of God does not receive adequate attention. I prefer to consider the manner of God's self-disclosure as Creator, Redeemer, and Reconciler. Although these descriptive terms should not limit our understanding of God, they can help us focus on God's nurturing and providential care of human beings. Schubert Ogden is critical of liberation theologians for not emphasizing the metaphysical attributes of God. I reverse this criticism: Traditional theology has had too much to say about God's metaphysical attributes and too little to say about God's work of liberation. We must ask the following questions: What has God revealed regarding creation, redemption, and reconciliation? What does this divine revelation imply regarding human liberation?

The saving knowledge we have through Christ is key to understanding God's work of liberation. The Christian God is a triune God, a unity-in-trinity and a trinity-in-unity. What one thinks of Christ is an important concern, for it is in and through Christ that we know God best. The mind and will of God is revealed through Christ. Both the humanity and divinity of Christ are precious to the believer.

An Africentric Perspective on Christology

Some approaches to Christology begin with the Cross and Resurrection. Little attention is given to the earthly life of Jesus. Black religion, insofar as the acceptance of the Christian revelation is concerned, has paid strong attention to the place of Jesus in the believer's life. Being treated so inhumanely by other human beings, African American Christians see Jesus as a divine friend to whom they could turn in the time of trouble.

In *Black Religion,* Joseph Washington emphasized the central place of Jesus in black faith:

> In order to meet the Underground Railroad and escape the cruelty of the overseers, Negroes found it advantageous to:
>
> > Steal away, steal away
> > Steal away to Jesus,
> > Steal away, steal away home,
> > I ain't got long to stay here.[1]

In fact, as Washington describes black religion, it might well be called Jesusology. He argued that we had no substantial theology or ecumenical vision.

Gayraud S. Wilmore reminds us that the concept of the black Messiah has been around a long time. As early as 1829 Robert Alexander Young spoke of a Christ figure who would champion the cause of the "degraded of the earth." The author goes on to say that the black Messiah has been mentioned by Africans of the African diaspora ever since.[2]

In 1949, long before the recent black theology movement, the mystic and religious philosopher Howard Thurman wrote a classic statement on the place of Jesus among black believers. However, insofar as Christology in the black church tradition is concerned, this volume still holds its own. *Jesus and the Disinherited* has claimed the attention of black ministers and religious scholars since it was written. Thurman seems to have captured the essence of the meaning of Jesus for black believers. Martin Luther King Jr. is reported to have carried this volume with him as he traveled.

In a conversation with me in his San Francisco residence, Thurman said he has little regard for christological dogmas, whether ancient or modern. He said: "I want to get to Jesus as soon as possible!" For Thurman, Christology is limited primarily to what theologians refer to as the Jesus of history. He was devoted to the human Jesus who identified with "the disinherited," men and women with their backs against the wall.[3]

Albert B. Cleage Jr. initiated the more recent discussion in his *Black Messiah*,[4] where he spoke of a literal "black Christ." Tracing the long series of persons in Jesus' Jewish lineage, Cleage claimed that Jesus is of African ancestry. Thurman spoke of the Jewishness of Jesus, but Cleage proclaimed his blackness. Most theologians, myself included, did not accept Cleage's literal black Messiah. I opted for a psychosocial meaning of the notion but held firmly to Thurman's emphasis upon the human Jesus. As I discovered Dietrich Bonhoeffer's emphasis on the humanity of Jesus, my version was deepened and sharpened. His Jesus "the man for others," whose life is in solidarity with our lives from "the crib to the cross," became an excellent statement of what the human Jesus means to a suffering race.[5]

The writings of the late Bishop Joseph A. Johnson Jr., a New Testament theologian and prelate of the C.M.E. Church, are no less compelling. Johnson did not rest with the humanity of Jesus, as important as that identity is. We also need a "Christ of faith," by which I mean the divinity of Christ, his saviorhood. All have sinned and need redemption from sin. Sinful human beings, regardless of race or condition, are in need of human role models. They need persons of noble character to point the way to a life of righteousness.

We must affirm the humanity of Jesus, for the human Jesus is the best example of moral excellence that has ever appeared in history. We should familiarize ourselves with the life of Jesus from crib to cross. He was born in a barn. He was wrapped in a blanket used to keep sick cattle warm. The shepherds welcomed his birth. Herod sought to do away with the infant Jesus. Nonetheless, for the poor, he was the long-awaited Messiah who had come to set his people free.

In his life and ministry, Jesus identified with the least, the lonely, and the lost. Jesus states his call to minister in Luke 4:18 when he reads a passage of ancient Scripture from the book of Isaiah: "The Spirit of the Lord is upon me." Yet the religious establishment despised him. Jesus was misunderstood because he did his work among those who were ostracized by good, respectable, religious people. He worked among the downcast, the nobodies of his day. He went about doing good. Wherever he went the sick were healed, the lame walked, the deaf could hear, and the dead were raised. The poor heard the gospel preached to them.

Jesus is so precious to black Christians that some have described black religion as Jesusology. Jesus is loved because he cares. He is a friend to the friendless and Savior to the lost. Thus, not only black theologians but also theologians of liberation in the Southern Hemisphere speak of Jesus as Liberator. Jesus means freedom to the oppressed. However, it is important to say also that the Jesus of history is the Christ of faith. We humans need not merely a good moral example but a Savior. The resources we require, the strength we need is not in us.

Søren Kierkegaard once compared Jesus with Socrates, a great moral philosopher who taught us how to think. He insisted that virtue is knowledge and knowledge virtue, and he gave his life as a testimony to his dedication to truth and goodness. Kierkegaard observed that we could study the life and thought of Socrates but would not need to know Socrates as a person. Instead, we could embrace the truth that Socrates taught through our power of thought. But the encounter with Jesus, *the Truth*, is of a different order: salvation requires a personal encounter with Jesus. One has to decide what to do with Jesus. He makes a claim upon our lives. Jesus calls us to a relationship with God. Through Jesus we are called to decision and summoned to a costly discipleship. Our eternal salvation depends upon our relation to God in Christ. This is not a cultural enrichment experience — it is a matter of our salvation. His name shall be called Jesus, for he shall save his people from their sins.

We must be concerned with the Christ of faith as well as the Jesus of history. We must inquire about the manner in which the Incarnation manifests the nature, life, and will of God. We must finally consider the way in which Jesus Christ overcomes sin and evil through his cross, resurrection, and ascension. The incarnated Lord is the crucified and resurrected One. Incarnation and atonement are united in Jesus as the Christ.

A well-grounded Christology is a necessary foundation for thinking about Christ in any cultural context. With these insights before us, we can meaningfully understand the black Messiah and are able to see the face of Christ and to image Jesus in our racial, cultural, social, or ethnic context. This perception is in a manner that brings Christ, the revealer of God, powerfully and savingly into our midst, into our lives.

John Mackay wrote a powerful book about the interpretation of Christ that Christians from Spain and Portugal introduced to the Latin American Indians. In *The Spanish Christ,* the author describes the difference between the Christ of the colonists who were masters over Indian peasants and African slaves and the Christ they presented to the powerless. The Christ of the powerful in church and state was exalted and magisterial, so high as to be unreachable. (This is the reason that the cult of Mary developed. Mary, as mother of Jesus, became the mediatrix. Through the compassion of Mary, her Son could be reached.) The Christ of the poor was one who suffered with them. This Christ hangs on the cross, unable to assist the powerless. This Christ shares their pain but is not in a position to alleviate their suffering. On the one hand, Christ is in heaven. On the other hand, Christ is on the cross. For those who suffer oppression there is Good Friday but no Easter.

The Puritans introduced to black slaves in the United States a different image of Christ. However, this Christ was too sentimental and otherworldly to assist in their liberation. Even today, some white evangelicals proclaim a Jesus "meek and mild" who does not come to set the oppressed free. Jesus is not the Liberator. For more than two hundred years there has been a rejection of this version of the person and place of Jesus Christ. While some have accepted this interpretation, the black church tradition as a whole questions it.

During the peak period of the discussions of the black Messiah, I became sensitive to the one-sided manner Jesus as the Christ had been presented aesthetically and theologically. The "White-Americanized-Christ," as Vincent Harding described him, has no resemblance to black people and their condition as they experienced racial oppression. There was no cultural affinity with nonwhites anywhere in the world.

As I moved about in the black churches and communities, I saw that black Christians lacked psychological and cultural affinity with this Eurocentric Christ. If Christ, as Kierkegaard implied, should be our contemporary, then we should be able to observe his image and cry out: "My Lord and my God!" When we ask Bonhoeffer's question, "What is the meaning of Christ for us today?" we must answer that the traditional image of Christ advanced by Eurocentric theologians has little existential meaning for us. The Christ of each people or person is likewise a universal savior. However, the "eachness" of his saviorhood precedes the "allness" of his redeemership. Much of the discussion concerning the black Messiah also has real meaning in the Africentric focus for theological reflection. Through this understanding of Jesus Christ, one is able to see the color of God.

The Spirit of God in Our Midst

As we think of God, we must consider the work of the Holy Spirit in our personal lives and in the church. The presence of the Spirit is powerfully manifest in the celebration of the gospel in black churches. The Spirit is present in music, prayers, praise, and sermon. This means that greater attention needs to be given to our interpretation of the Holy Spirit. Pentecostalism is a movement in Africultures worldwide. Whereas other Christians may have to deal with the absence of the Spirit, African peoples must be concerned with the Spirit's overwhelming presence.

The Church of God in Christ, a black pentecostal denomination in the United States, is the fastest growing religious body among black Christians. Nevertheless, thus far its leaders have not done much to provide a serious theological basis for this denomination. This needs to be done, since the "spirits need to be tried" or examined to see if they be of God. This important doctrine related to the understanding of God will need to be treated by black theologians, even if Pentecostals do not assume this important task. Black theologians will need direction, guidance, and understanding.

The Holy Spirit is a Person, a mode of divine being and God's revelation of Godself in the form of spirit. Spirit can be everywhere without being everything. The Holy Spirit is our Teacher, Comforter, Guide, and Strengthener. The Holy Spirit is the One who brooded over the chaos that became a cosmos by God's creative act. The Holy Spirit is the One who gave utterance to the prophets of Israel, among them Amos, Micah, and Isaiah. The Holy Spirit rested upon Jesus as he emerged from the waters of baptism. The Holy Spirit was poured forth at Pentecost, giving birth to the Christian church. The Spirit informed Peter and influenced Paul as apostles of the Good News from God through Christ. Jesus Christ also sends the Holy Spirit.

Christology and pneumatology must be brought together in the Christian understanding of God. God was in Christ reconciling the world to Godself. Yet, we must also say that the Lord is the Spirit. The Christ-mysticism of the apostle Paul is instructive. He asserts that his life is hid in Christ in God. Where the Spirit of the Lord is, there is liberty. Paul further states that whether he lives or dies, he remains in Christ. It is also important, according to Paul, to assert that one observes the "fruits of the Spirit" where the light, life, and love of God are revealed with power and presence through Christ and the agency of the Holy Spirit.

As we search our ancestral roots, we find that a spiritual presence is evident in the religion of African cultures. We therefore need to know if this spiritual presence is from God. We have stated some ways in which observations of the character of spiritual presence can be measured. We need to inquire if the spiritual presence bears marks of the character of God we meet in Jesus as the Christ.

When we ask about the color of God, we are inquiring if God enters into our midst as a salvific reality. We are asking if God understands our language, our needs, and our longings. Does God love us as a people? Does God love us as individual persons? Does God in the threefold revelation as Father, Son, and Holy Spirit care about our situation and our needs? Does God encounter us where we are in order to sustain, comfort, heal, redeem, and sanctify us as heirs of the promised kingdom? If we can understand God as One who relates to us and we to God, we are on the threshold of a discovery of the color of God.

The insights introduced in this chapter are not a comprehensive systematic theology based upon Africentric reflections. They are basic insights introduced as foundational for this attempt to demonstrate how the Africentric outlook may enrich and empower the understanding and living of our Christian faith, especially in ministry and worship. In our next chapter we will further explore this relationship as we describe two celebrations — one Christian and the other Africentric. We refer to Christmas and Kwanzaa.

Notes

1. Joseph Washington Jr., *Black Religion* (Boston: Beacon: 1964), 211.
2. Gayraud S. Wilmore, *Black Religion and Black Radicalism*, 3rd ed. (Maryknoll, N.Y.: Orbis, 1984), 37.
3. Howard Thurman, *Jesus and the Disinherited* (Richmond, Ind.: Friend's Press, 1981).
4. Albert B. Cleage Jr., *The Black Messiah* (New York: Sheed and Ward, 1969).
5. Dietrich Bonhoeffer, *Christ the Center* (New York: Harper, 1978).

Chapter 6

Africentric Culture and Christian Theology

A CHRISTMAS BENEDICTION

The real work of Christmas begins when Christmas Day is over, as Christ's great mission was accomplished long after the day of his birth. What we do at Christmastime for the hungry, the illclothed [*sic*] and poorly housed, the lonely, the sick and the sad will bless them and be good for us, but Christmas-time [*sic*] goodness is only a cattle-stall start. What counts most is what the memory of Christ's coming does for our "ordinary" days.

Now may the meaning of Christmas fall upon your mind and spirit like autumn leaves upon the waiting soil. May the Christmas gospel mix with all your thoughts and desires, your values and purposes, until you are thoroughly enriched and until you grow an abundance of Christlike graces that produce Christlike deeds. Amen.

— HAROLD KOHN
The European Evangelist 43, no. 4 (winter 1998)

BRINGING TOGETHER Christian theology and African culture, I offer in this chapter a discussion that builds a bridge over which one may travel through culture to faith. This discussion is crucial to our reflection on the relation of Africentrism and faith. It critically examines the meaning of culture and the nature of our Christian confession. Culture and the Christian faith are not identical, but they can be meaningfully related. The relationship between culture and faith may be noted by contrasting the celebrations of Christmas and Kwanzaa. Christmas, when properly celebrated, lifts up the birth of our Savior. Kwanzaa, by contrast, has profound meaning for African Americans, both believers and nonbelievers, as a major cultural celebration. Christmas puts us directly in touch with the essence of our faith. Kwanzaa lifts up the substance of our cultural heritage, even our Africentric roots. Reflecting on these two celebrations, their origin, and their meaning can provide some direction to devout Christian believers of African American descent.

To whom does Christmas belong? This inquiry is an Africentric question, and the answer to it sets the mood for an Africentric perspective.

The unusually warm temperature during December 1998, almost nationwide, dampened what some call the mood of Christmas. We have associated Christmas with the climate in the North Atlantic countries. The celebration of this holy season has been identified with the ability to exchange often expensive material gifts with family members and friends. In our Christmas celebration we have made Christ a captive to a particular culture. This westernization process carries over even into our dress and images of the season. Santa Claus is usually a white male. Children of all racial and ethnic backgrounds have a whitened image of the person at the center of the Christmas celebration. As Vincent Harding once observed, even the Savior is portrayed as "a white Americanized Christ."

The songs we sing also bear the message that Christmas belongs to those who live in places where December has a cold climate. For anyone spending a period of time in a tropical country or a country south of the equator, the message of most of our carols must appear strange and out of place. Christ and Christmas in the United States have been both commercialized and Europeanized.

Christ is the one who brings meaning to Christmas. The saviorhood of this person is the meaning of Christmas, which is centered on the Savior's birth. This season has everything to do with the redemption of sinful humanity. The advent of Christ is the fulfillment of God's salvific promise to mend a broken relationship with God. It is not a process of acculturation. Christ, "the desire of all nations," does not belong to a particular people but to all peoples. Therefore, it is improper to associate his coming and his presence with only one culture as a medium through which God's saving revelation may be manifest. Culture can be a medium, but it is not the message God gives us in Jesus as the Christ.

Culture, the context in which individuals are socialized, has a history and bears a heritage. Culture helps to shape our life view and worldview. It is our *Lebenswelt*, our living world. The significance of culture is intergenerational, sustaining values that parents share with their children. Many intellectual and literary devices are used to pass from one generation to another the knowledge of life born of experience. Mythology, folklore, stories, poetry, and many other means of communication are used to pass cultural traits down through history. All people, including Africans and African Americans, have a culture. For African Americans faith and culture meet in Christmas and Kwanzaa.

A Foundational Assumption: Culture and Christianity Are Not Identical

Culture and Christianity are not identical. Christianity is neither bound to any particular culture nor tied to any particular culture's customs and traditions. From the Christian perspective we are concerned with Christology, the person and work of Christ. For Christians there is no Christmas without Christ. Christ himself is the meaning of Christmas.

Christianity has its own value system, its own history. It lays a claim upon its adherents to bring to any and all cultures a critical stance of judgment. It does not conform to any particular culture but transforms culture according to its confessional demands. However, the Christian faith may find a particular cultural trait or event to be a meaningful vehicle of expression. We can see how Kwanzaa has this potential when we examine Kwanzaa and Christmas for Christian believers.

Culture as the Context of Theology

Culture is important to theology, but it does not replace theology. Kwanzaa is Africentric, while Christmas is Christocentric. In *God of the Oppressed*, James Cone observes, "Unless we black theologians can make an adequate distinction between divine revelation and human aspirations, there is nothing to keep black theology from identifying God's will with anything black people should decide to do at any given historical moment."[1]

In his next paragraph, Cone discusses the relation between theology and culture, comparing his insights with H. Richard Niebuhr's *Christ and Culture*. Niebuhr affirms the universal claims of divine revelation in Jesus Christ, a revelation that is said to transcend the limitation of history. But Niebuhr recognized that human speech about divine revelation is conditioned by culture and history. Divine revelation is universal, but theological talk about revelation is particular.

Niebuhr in *Christ and Culture* has delineated five typologies in the relationship between Christ and culture.[2] The first stance, that of radical Christians, sets Christ in opposition to culture and absolutizes the authority of Christ over Christians. Everything cultural is said to be anti-Christian, so one rejects cultural claims and withdraws from culture.

In the second stance, Christ is related to culture. For instance, we cannot deny the Jewishness of Jesus. He is part of a social heritage that is transmitted and passed on.

Christ is above culture in the third stance. Those who hold this view insist that it is not possible to blend God's work and human effort. This would reduce the infinite to the finite and absolutize what is relative.

The dramatic position is the fourth stance, in which the choice is between God and self. Grace is in God, and sin is in humans. Christians are redeemed but also sinners. Martin Luther held the view that Christians are redeemed sinners. God calls Christians to obedience in culture, sustaining them in the context of its corruption. Niebuhr also attributes this paradoxical view to Søren Kierkegaard.

The fifth view is the conversionist type, which defines Christ as the transformer of culture. It is affirmative and hopeful toward culture. The conversionist lives in an openness for the divine future breaking into the human present transforming human culture into the glory of God.[3] This "Christ the transformer of culture" is the typology most instructive for us. Christianity is at its most powerful mode of explanation when faith stands above and over against culture as a transcendent form of judgment. Such judgment is characteristic of the great prophets of Israel and in Jesus. Martin Luther King Jr. illustrated for African Americans how this view is manifest.

Since my concern is not identical with Cone's, I do not pursue his critique of Niebuhr here. The issues raised seems to confirm several insights concerning the social location and determination of thought, including theological reflection. Social reality precedes thinking. Our task is not to admit the social/cultural considerations alone. Christians have a transcendent norm based upon our acceptance of the revelation of God in Christ.

According to Niebuhr, culture is bound up with human life in society. That is to say, culture is social. It is the social heritage that individuals receive, use, and pass along. In the second instance, culture is human achievement and the world of values. It comes into being to serve human purposes and goals. Culture nourishes life, but it also imposes burdens upon it. Niebuhr rightly observes that these characteristics of culture lay claims on us even as we attempt to live under the authority of Jesus Christ. Christians must live in the world, but Christians must not be of the world. Christ and culture are in tension. Maintaining our proper balance and perspective demands a constant dialogue.[4]

The issue before us is the relationship between an Africentric and a Christocentric life. We are seeking a life view and worldview, culturally speaking, in which to affirm our faith in Christ and our witness in Christian community, the church. How may we as a people affirm our heritage, going back to our classical African roots, and at the same time be authentic followers of Christ? Kwanzaa and Christmas, though usually viewed as events or celebrations, are powerful symbols of the tension between Africentrism and Christocentrism.

In this case we have in mind symbol or symbolic language as used by Paul Tillich, John Macquarrie, and others who use symbolic language to explain the essential doctrines of the faith. A symbol is a way of speaking of something or viewing something, where our use of a word or event participates in what it expresses but also points above and beyond the word or event itself. For instance, consider the flag of a nation. A flag may appear to be cloth with stars and stripes, but if it is attacked during war on the high seas, it symbolizes a nation under fire. A flag has meaning not in itself but in the national life to which it points. In this manner, we have used Kwanzaa and Christmas to symbolize a perspective on black life, one cultural and one religious.

When we celebrate Kwanzaa, we pay respect to an august heritage of African people on the continent and throughout the African diaspora. When we celebrate Christmas, we lift up the Christian message of redemption. Both Kwanzaa and Christmas can have rich and empowering meanings for black people. How then do we bring these meanings into concert with each other without losing or distorting either?

Kwanzaa and Christmas

Kwanzaa is an African American celebration that takes place between Christmas and New Year. For some it is a cultural celebration only that does not replace Christmas. However, for others it is celebrated in the place of Christmas. Kwanzaa is also on the borderline, and for some it can become a quasi-religious event and appear to be an acceptable replacement for Christmas. Attractive and eventful, Kwanzaa can have profound meaning for all Africans in the African diaspora. If our Christian roots are not deep, it can easily appear to be all that is necessary during this season. The fact that it is held during Christmas week makes its purpose suspect.

Kwanzaa was initiated by Maulana Ron-Karenga, a political activist and a cultural anthropologist. During the late 1960s he openly criticized Christianity as "spookism." Brought up as a Baptist, he was in open rebellion against the church. It seems clear that his negative attitude toward Christianity and Jesus, who for him was a "dead Jew," may have been in his mind when he established Kwanzaa.

Since the establishment of Kwanzaa, Karenga has embraced a more substantive religious system. However, he turned not to Christianity but to ancient Egypt for a religious faith. He now stresses that Kwanzaa is purely cultural and is not anti-Christian or anti-Muslim, further insisting that African people regardless of their political persuasion or religious beliefs should observe Kwanzaa. This turn of events is not helpful to devout Christians who see benefits in the celebration of Kwanzaa but who do not see the need of abandoning their faith in Jesus Christ in order to do so. While keeping in mind these concerns about the origin and celebration of Kwanzaa, we need to consider the positive benefits African American Christians may receive through participation in this cultural event.

Kwanzaa is based upon seven principles of nationhood: history, mythology, creative motif, ethos, social organization, political organization, and economic organization.[5] Kwanzaa, celebrated by about eighteen million people each year, spans the last week of December and culminates on New Year's Day.

Kwanzaa means "first" in Swahili, for the first fruits of the year. The first harvest has been a time of celebration for Africans since the beginnings of agriculture. Each night a candle is lit representing one of the seven principles of Nguzo Saba, of the holiday season. Karenga selected these principles because they are common in African history. Swahili, the most common African language, is used to identify them. They are as follows:

> *Umoja* — unity
> *Kujichagulia* — self-determination
> *Ujima* — collective work and responsibility
> *Nia* — purpose
> *Kuumba* — creativity
> *Imani* — faith

The purpose of the event is to build family, community, and culture. For instance, the principle of cooperative economics is intended to encourage black people to create their own businesses and to spend their money at black-owned stores.

A set of meaningful symbols is associated with the celebration of Kwanzaa. The unity cup points to the need to come together. The black, red, and green flag is a powerful cluster of meaning. Black is for the people, red for struggle, and green for hope. In the United States the holiday consists of a synthesis of African and African American traditions. These traditions emphasize respect for the physical environment and commitment to truth and justice. Karenga based his conclusions upon research of cultures spanning the African continent, but he also acknowledges the influence of the black power movement of the 1960s — a renaissance of awareness among African Americans — upon his outlook. He stresses the need for education; education, he observes, is rooted in African tradition. Knowledge is a moral requirement.

The celebration was begun in 1966 with the support of US, a group of Karenga's colleagues based in Los Angeles that is committed to learning about African history and teaching it to African Americans. After being taught about the idea of Kwanzaa, the members of US traveled around the country and promoted it until many African Americans accepted it as a cultural event. Although Kwanzaa began as an organizational expression, within two years it found popular acclaim. First it was a local community phenomenon, and then it spread nationwide. It met the need in the people of African descent to reaffirm their roots. Some fear that its very purpose may be diluted by its popularity. Karenga believes that the more the celebration is embraced, the more black people will be enriched and empowered by participating in it.[6]

Christmas is one of two great celebrations on the annual program in Christian churches, only Easter being comparable with the event honoring Christ's birth. The birth of Christ is a pivotal event in Christian history and in the personal life of Christians. Although this event has been trivialized and commercialized, the true meaning of Christmas has to do with the birth of Jesus, the Christ Child. Christ *is* Christmas.

The feasting and exchanging of gifts are not significant if Christ is not at the center of the Christmas event. Karl Barth was correct, I believe, when he observed that "we ought to sing Easter Hymns at Christmas." He was pointing to the awesome salvific nature of the advent of the Savior. The message of Christmas is expressed in this key exaltation: "His name shall be called Jesus, for he shall save his people from their sins."

If Christmas is properly understood and observed, there is no danger that a mere cultural event can replace or supplant Christmas in the life experience of a devout Christian. Kwanzaa can never replace the redemptive significance of Christmas. Nonetheless, African American Christians can embrace the African cultural heritage celebrated in Kwanzaa. We can benefit from nurturing our youth on the values Kwanzaa promotes, and we can do so without excessive concerns about the fact that this celebration may have originated in less than ideal circumstances.

Kwanzaa can be scheduled after a proper celebration of Christmas. Even the gifts shared during the Kwanzaa week must be handmade and do not duplicate gifts shared at Christmas. These gifts demonstrate one of the principles of Kwanzaa, that of creativity. The celebration of Kwanzaa is not inconsistent with Christian beliefs or practices. It does not take the place of our celebration of Christmas. Indeed, the following chapters may indicate additional ways in which Kwanzaa and other practices and customs adapted from Africa are not only consistent with our Christian faith but also useful in faith's expression and practice. If we can lift these two celebrations to their highest level of meaning, they will complement each other and bring enrichment and empowerment to African American personal and communal living. The celebration of Kwanzaa illustrates how Africentrism offers means by which Christian ministers can address personal and community needs. Two conclusions may be drawn from examining Christmas and Kwanzaa: First, the values, ideals, and celebration of Kwanzaa do not conflict with the Christian faith; and second, the celebration of Kwanzaa may be a useful ministry to African Americans. The next chapter elaborates on this latter crucial point, that is, that Africentrism can provide avenues for ministry and service with African American Christians.

Notes

1. James Cone, *God of the Oppressed* (New York: Seabury, 1975), 84–85.

2. H. Richard Niebuhr, *Christ and Culture* (New York: Harper, 1956), 41–45.

3. Cone, 75–91.

4. Niebuhr, 39.

5. See Molefi Kete Asante, *Afrocentricity* (Trenton, N.J.: African World Press, 1989), 19–21.

6. This capsule of Karenga's understanding of Kwanzaa was compiled by Michael Laplar in *The Chronicle of Higher Education* (December 14, 1994), A7. Cf. Angela Shelf Medearis, *The Seven Days of Kwanzaa* (New York: Scholastic, 1994).

Chapter 7

Africentric Culture and Christian Ministry

AS SERVANTS IN A SERVANT CHURCH, we are called to a ministry of liberation and reconciliation in the church of Jesus Christ. In sum we are to be servants of the word. Sometimes that word disturbs, and sometimes it heals. Jesus Christ is the Great Shepherd of the sheep, and as ministers we are privileged to serve in the awesome role of undershepherds. We serve under divine guidance as agents of God's salvific purpose among human beings.

This reflection on ministry moves us to apply theology to grassroots witness and service. We are concerned with the manner in which we live out the faith. Therefore, as congregational leaders — clerical and lay — we need to be concerned about the nature of our responsibility and how we carry it out.

In this chapter on an Africentric perspective on ministry, I discuss in some detail the relation between Christianity and culture with ministry in mind. An Africentric ministry is described in terms of its benefits by relating it to two principles of Kwanzaa. The values of Kwanzaa are analyzed in two categories: personal awareness and communal consciousness. I use the notion of the black church as an extended family to focus upon the African roots inherent in the black church tradition and the Africentric ministry of healing and outreach. Finally I deal with the need for self-esteem in both its individual and communal expression as I attempt to show how the Africentric perspective can greatly enhance this virtue in African Americans. I am especially concerned as to how the linkage between the faith and Africentrism can aid this process.

Culture as the Context of Christian Ministry

The section referring to Niebuhr's typology (see chap. 6) clarifies the proper distinction between theology and culture. From that discussion I concluded that salvation comes through faith that is not dependent upon our accepting all the customs and traditions of any particular culture. However, ministry must take place in a cultural context. The context can be monocultural or cross-cultural, but humans are always located in a cultural setting. Some additional discussion about Christianity's relation to culture can illuminate the Christian's perspective for ministry within a culture.

Anthropologist Charles H. Kraft in *Christianity in Culture* outlines two "God in culture" positions.[1] He lays a foundation for his discussion by posing a question: "Is God the originator of culture?" He also formulates a "God against culture" position. God, he concludes, created people with the capacity and the need for culture.

Viewing culture from a Christian point of view, Kraft sees the cultural structuring of human behavior or the capacity for producing culture "as a provision of a loving God for human well-being." He observes that humans who are dysfunctional do not have clearly defined and consistent guidelines for behavior on both a personal and a social level. He will not accept the view that God is against culture, because that view insists that Christians should withdraw from culture, that they should reject, escape, isolate, and insulate themselves from the world in order to obtain holiness and procure ultimate salvation. For Kraft the Christian way is to pledge allegiance to God and then use culture for him.

Escape from culture is difficult since culture is around us and within us. We can, however, innovate, replace, add to, transform, and in other ways alter our use of the culture received. Christians often find it necessary to transform culture as they make use of it for God's kingdom's sake. Christians therefore should not view culture as inherently evil. It is to be seen more as an instrument to be used for a salvific purpose.

Kraft describes two "God in culture" positions. The first is the group that sees God (or Christ) as a cultural hero. Human longing is deified. God is created in our image. For instance, some Americans so focus on the idealized love of God that they are not able to see that

God is our Judge as well as our Creator and Redeemer. Compare this with the early Hebrew culture, in which the majesty and righteousness of God obscured his loving-kindness and tender mercy.

Others who see God in culture view God as endorsing one particular culture. American civil religion (the "God and country" syndrome) illustrates this view, as does any position that exalts "a tribal god."[2] We are dangerously close to this position in the marriage between conservative religion and conservative politics. Some people see this religiopolitical alliance as the only road to acceptable family values and the democratic-capitalist perspective. For them, it is not only the basis for the American way of life but also the foundation of "a new world order." It is obvious that some of these insights come from Kraft, but it is also my interpretation. It may take Kraft beyond where he is willing to go.

Although Kraft describes five positions of the "God above culture" typology, I will mention only the fifth, a "God above but through culture" position. Culture may be understood as an integrated pattern of human knowledge, belief, and behavior that depends upon human capacities to learn and pass on these traits to future generations. Culture may be said to be a set of customary beliefs, social forms, and material traits of a particular ethnic, racial, religious, or social group.[3]

With this formal understanding of culture, we come to our conclusion on God and culture. Kraft views culture as neither an enemy nor a friend of God or humans. Instead, culture is something to be used by personal beings, by God and humans. It is the milieu in which all encounters with or between human beings take place and the terms by which all human understanding and maturation occur. The human psyche is structured by culture, as is every social group — family, community, church.[4]

Culture is a kind of road map to get people where they need to go, and the form and functions of culture may be said to be neutral with respect to God and humans. Cultures set patterns, organizations, and structures for living. These aspects of culture, and culture itself, are not inherently evil or good. Human beings, however, are infected with sin. Cultures are also affected by human sin. Meanings intended and meanings received are tainted by sin. We are also imperfect, finite, and limited in understanding. Human beings, therefore, improperly use culture.

The Christian faith insists we are redeemable. As a result, redeemed human beings begin to do things differently. Redeemed persons use cultural traits differently, for they have a new allegiance and a new master. When individuals are changed, they can engage in the transformation of culture. The structures in which persons live are subject to change. When groups of people undergo redemptive transformation, greater impact can be seen in cultural change. Thus when such transformation takes place as the result of a relationship with God, we may rightly speak of the influence of God upon cultural change.

God is eternal and exists outside of culture. However, God chooses the cultural context as the arena of interaction with people, often using human agency and language to intervene in human affairs. The language through which God speaks participates fully in human culture with all its strengths and weaknesses. This is illustrated by God's encounter with Israel through Hebrew language and culture. Jesus and his disciples operated in Aramaic culture and language. When the New Testament was recorded for a Greek-speaking audience, Greek was employed. Greek culture also became the cultural medium through which the gospel was communicated to the Greco-Roman/Gentile world. God has shown through the biblical record a determination to communicate a saving revelation to different segments of humanity within their own linguistic and cultural contexts. Kraft correctly concludes: "God is absolute and finite. Yet, He had freely chosen to employ human culture; and, at major points, to limit himself to the capacities of culture in his interaction with people."[5]

I have insisted upon the importance of culture, but I have clearly distinguished between culture and redemption. Christians, it seems to me, are forced to consider culture as their context for the life of faith and witness. However, they are not in a position to substitute culture for an affirmation of faith. This discussion is important for our Africentric approach to Christian mission and ministry. For those who minister in the church of Jesus, Christian culture is the medium and not the message.

On Church and Ministry

The church is in the world but not of the world. It has the task of transforming the world without losing itself in the world. The church is God's human colony, always in danger of cultural captivity. If, however, the church becomes a captive to culture, it loses its redemptive power.

A good example of this tragic condition is what happened to the state church in Germany during World War II. The German Christians endorsed Hitler and entered into an unholy alliance with Nazism. Karl Barth and Dietrich Bonhoeffer formed the Confessional Church, which launched a systematic assault upon the established church.

During the period of black slavery in the United States and during the apartheid era in South Africa, Christians and churches lived in a state of apostasy against the true nature and mission of the church of Jesus Christ. Insofar as racism, sexism, and other forms of injustice prevail in our houses of worship, we are not in a state of grace. We languish in cultural captivity and have little redemptive significance. Although the examples listed are extreme, it is time nevertheless to issue a word of caution for those who so glibly endorse African-centeredness. Africentricity must not replace Christ-centeredness.

We can make good use of our rich and august culture. Certain aspects of Africentricity can greatly enrich and empower the mission and ministry of our churches. It is clear from a Christian theological perspective that our people still need more than culture for their salvation.

I recall a powerful reflection on the Christian faith by a Catholic layperson. When Fr. Stallings, now archbishop, initiated his movement in Washington, I asked my longtime musician friend if he was going to leave his congregation and join Stallings' Imani Temple. Without hesitation, my friend responded that culture and redemption are two different things. His membership in the historic Catholic church has to do with his salvation. Later, as he lapsed into a coma and eventually died, his concern for eternal salvation took on even greater meaning in my reflections.

My friend was a lifelong teacher of black youth in high school and college. He was an expert on both Western classical music and African American music, both secular and sacred, and he placed great emphasis upon the cultural aspects of music. He was even thoroughly Africentric in his art, having spent most of his career in black institutions. It was the more profound that he was clearly able to see that his Christian faith transcended his cultural affinity. He clearly illustrates for me the possibility of having the right perspective on the concerns before us.

It is quite in order for African Americans to be Africentric in outlook. They may even have a passion for lifting up their rich cultural heritage. It is a categorical misunderstanding, however, when we attempt to be Africentric without having faith in God or to substitute culture for redemption. My example should not be taken as a tirade against Fr. Stallings and his protest. I have written concerning racism in the Catholic church. I know there is a powerful incentive to renounce that church. I also believe that Stallings, according to his understanding, wants to combine culture and Christianity.

Ministry and mission are ways the church expresses itself in human affairs. In our churches, ministers place a strong emphasis upon a divine call. This is an august tradition. We also believe in mentoring those who are called. This too is a significant characteristic of our ministerial tradition. These aspects of ministry may not be unique to the black church, but they are worthy and should be retained. I can witness to the power of these traits of our ministerial tradition. Independent of protracted study, I am especially grateful that I had fathers in ministry who nurtured and guided me during the days of my youth. Now with large numbers of women in ministry, there is a need for mothers in ministry to mentor women. However, male ministers must also seek to share their experience with women entering ministry.

A few aspects of ministry may have cultural warrants, but a genuine ministry must be based upon the ministry of Jesus Christ as norm. With the New Testament understanding of the church as the extension of the Incarnation, we are able to view the church as a servant church. Ministry in the church of Jesus Christ through the agency of the Holy Spirit is a servant ministry.

In spite of all our pretensions, however, African Americans are likely to think "white" and aspire to Western values and the approval of those who seem to be in control. We have a subculture of survival, but it is fueled by values of success and consumption in the larger society. For the most part we do not know who we are or where we are going. Africentrism changes all that. We develop an African-centered personal and collective consciousness that gives us a sense of "somebodiness" grounded in our rich heritage.

Personal Awareness

Personal and communal awareness are two dimensions of Africentricity. An important dimension of freedom is psychological. It is possible to be conditioned in personal consciousness so as to be unaware that things can be different. During World War II, for example, the British took Jürgen Moltmann into prison. He tells that after a period he adjusted to his confinement and was contented, if not happy. His anxiety returned in full force when he heard he would be released within a few days. He observes that only when the prison doors open do one's chains begin to hurt.

In *Black Power,* Stokely Carmichael and Charles V. Hamilton insist that psychological freedom is a prerequisite for political freedom.[6] Carter G. Woodson made a similar observation, saying that if you control a black person's mind, you do not have to ask him or her to go to the back door; the person will find the door. No one is free until the mind is set free. Racism and colonialism had their greatest power through mind control.

Significantly, three of the seven principles of Kwanzaa — self-determination (*kujichagulia*), purpose (*nia*), and faith (*imani*) — focus upon personal transformation. I often recall how my parents prepared me to be inner-directed. This has served me well through the years. We will fail our children if we do not prepare them to be determined from within, for racism is still alive and well in this society.

In the late 1960s people talked a great deal about overcoming self-hatred. Persons who hate themselves are likely to hate those who look like them. The movie *Simple Justice* contains an account of Dr. Kenneth Clark, the black social scientist who administered the "doll test" to young black children. He placed a black doll and a white doll before them and then asked them several questions: Which doll is most beautiful? Which doll do you like? Which doll do you identify with? Which doll would you like to be like? Most black children saw the black doll as ugly and the white doll as beautiful. The black doll was undesirable, and the white doll was desirable. Though white lawyers called this "voodoo sociology," Thurgood Marshall and his legal team took Clark seriously. Clark's persistent use and interpretation of these tests assisted in the 1954 school desegregation victory.

The tests indicated that African American children are born into a society that attaches an inferiority tag to black skin and exalts white skin. One older girl taking the test caught herself endorsing the superiority of whiteness and asked to be excused because admitting what she had just said about herself and her people was too painful to accept or repeat.

Thus the cry "Black is beautiful" was a powerful message of personal liberation. Those who believed it had turned the tables upon the image of themselves in the minds of white people. They were now able to identify themselves. This creative self-definition gave them a new self-respect and a positive outlook on life. They had been reborn psychologically and could now look at themselves in the mirror and be proud. They could affirm their "somebodiness." They were then able to stand up to life.

We have made some gains during the years since the 1960s. The clock has recently been turned back. Africentrism has the promise of providing a powerful sense of self-esteem if it is properly understood. This can be a resource we need at this time. Without a sense of self-worth we will not be able to overcome the meaninglessness and despair in our streets. Our people, in order to thrive, need grounds for hope in their future and the future of their children.

Much of Africentrism is acceptable for our faith, but theologians and pastors must make the critical distinction between culture and redemption. Secular scholars, social scientists or educators, often identify religion with culture. We must be clear that for us no culture is a substitute for our faith. The "will to believe" is essential for our psychological well-being, as William James taught us. However, *imani*, the "faith" of Africentrism, is not the faith in Jesus Christ and the power of the Holy Spirit that redeems us from our sins and restores us to a proper salvific relation to God, Creator, Redeemer, and Sanctifier.

The Communal Consciousness and the Church as the Family of God

The remaining four principles of Kwanzaa lift up our life in community. We are psychosocial beings, persons in community. The principles remaining are unity, collective work and responsibility, cooperative economics, and creativity. *Umoja* (unity) indicates the need to work together in our families, communities, nation, and race. *Ujima* (collective work and responsibility) suggests that we team together to solve problems and to make our community a safe and productive place. *Ujamaa* (cooperative economics) refers to economic development, for instance, opening our own stores and other businesses and aiding each other to improve our financial position. *Kuumba* (creativity) taps into our giftedness in the arts and urges us to use our talents and our skills to make our community a better and more beautiful place in which to live. The African proverb, "I am because we are; because we are, I am" is a powerful expression of the group consciousness encouraged by these principles.

The sense of wholeness is characteristic of the cultural heritage of African Americans. This affirmation of group "belongingness" or solidarity carries over even to those who are outside the group — namely the unchurched or non-blood related African Americans. This group solidarity also extends to whites who are genuine in their friendship. This characteristic of the Africentric spirit is illustrated in wholesome relations within the African American family and church.

Ujamaa can mean "familyhood." Gabriel M. Setiloane of South Africa speaks of a saying *motho ke motho, ke batho* — Humans are humans in community. Humankind is humankind through other people.[7] The "family of God" image is useful in interpreting the nature and mission of black churches, although this understanding of the African American church is still underdeveloped in theology and ministerial practice. If it is understood and programmed, this image of the church can enrich and empower our people.

References to African proverbs and wise sayings in no way preempt the primacy of biblical warrants for our faith or the understanding of the nature and mission of the church. These sayings only illustrate the possibility of digging deep into our heritage to find resources for our life together in the body of Christ. Thus, in *Roots of a Black Future* I have interpreted the church using the image of the "extended family."[8] This very African notion antedates our time in slavery. In fact, recent studies find this sense of community in ancient Egypt long before the birth of Christ.

There is no reason why this communal notion of African life cannot enrich and empower the church for African American Christians. The church should be a caring, sharing community in which everybody is somebody. There is no reason why this sense of family should be locked up in the church. It should spill over into the community as we witness to "all sorts and conditions of people." In fact, this church of servanthood and compassion reaches in and beyond the black community. George Kelsey often has said that the black church is not a segregating church but the victim of segregation. It is the church of the "open door," willing and ready to minister to the need of the human family in Christ's name.

This tendency toward a sense of peoplehood is based upon compassion. It doesn't claim separatism or exclusive nationalism. It must be based ultimately upon a profound sense of self-esteem. This self-esteem may be developed by building upon the "Black is beautiful" theme of the recent black power movement. However, Africentrism provides a deeper meaning for our sense of self-worth, and to this aspect of our discussion we now turn our attention.

Africentrism and Self-Esteem

A missionary on furlough from his work in Argentina was visiting relatives in Miami. He boarded a bus, and a nine-year-old black boy took the vacant seat beside him. He was soon very comfortable holding a conversation with the boy and inquired of the boy what he desired for his life when he became a man. The boy, not answering him directly, said, "I wish I was white." A white man, the missionary realized that the boy suffered from a lack of self-esteem and did what he could to encourage the boy to be what he would like to be. The boy became very quiet and thoughtful. He left the bus without responding further to the missionary's encouraging remarks. The comment of the missionary to me was that he was disturbed by the fact that someone so young and bright had such low self-esteem.

This boy is not alone. This critical problem in African American families and communities is aborting the talent of so many of our black youth. In my visits with prisoners, I have found too many young black males behind bars because they have never thought well of themselves. The fact that so many of them have never related to a responsible father does not help. Some allow this abandonment by a father to lead them to believe that they are nobody. They ask, Why doesn't my father want me as a son? Why does he not love me?

Of course this lack of self-esteem can also be present among girls and young women. Though they may not be incarcerated, they may be walking the streets of our cities as prostitutes due to abuse by men or due to their lack of love from their fathers or mothers. This mistreatment and lack of care leads them to believe that they are not worthy of respect.

These circumstances present a great challenge for those of us who would be role models for scores of young people and adults who have been beaten down by circumstances. Lack of education and job opportunities can cause one to lose self-respect. Homelessness can increase the sense of being a nobody. All around us are people alone in this world with a sense that no one cares for them as a dignified person. Although persons of any race or ethnic group can experience a lack, in this society the pain is more intense if one adds racism to the poverty.

Our task as members of the body of Christ is to assure all sorts and conditions of persons that they are valued, they are made in God's image. "God loves you and so do I" must not be a trite statement but an expression of real compassion, supported by an effort to uplift those who have lost their sense of worth.

Persons who believe that they are down and out because they are black usually think that if they could be white their problems would be solved. Our society communicates this false aspiration to young black people. It says that if you are black there are few avenues out of your misery. You can be a great athlete or entertainer. Other ways are not abundant.

Africentrism assures black youth that they come from a noble heritage. They need not be filled with self-hate. It is true that we were slaves and that the shadow of slavery still lingers in the form of discrimination. However, one can still affirm a sense of self-worth and move forward against all odds. By combining the Christian faith claim that we are made in the image of God with a sense of belonging to a noble race, we may be able to lift up our heads and aspire for a better and brighter future.

The psychological victory prepares one to attain a concrete goal for one's life. With a made-up mind and a belief that we are somebody, African Americans can win many wonderful victories.

Africentrism and People Affirmation

A sense of heritage and solidarity is important for an oppressed group. Communalism, deeply grounded in our African roots, need not mean the exclusion of others from a different background, but it does mean that one is certain of one's own self and one's heritage. It means that one is safe and secure concerning who one is and the community of one's origin and upbringing. In affirming one's peoplehood, one is able to relate to other groups and to share the values of one's own community with others. One may still receive enrichment from outside. However, one never needs or desires to forsake one's own people in order to relate to another heritage or culture. Pride of one's culture, heritage, or race is a basis for a healthy and whole relationship with others.

As Søren Kierkegaard said, "Life is lived forward, but life is understood backward." Kierkegaard was referring to the individual's life, but I would like to apply this statement to the history of a people. "Who we are is who we were" is an insight I gleaned from reading Alexs Pate's *Amistad*. The African maxim "Because I am we are; and because we are, I am" also brings to mind the sense of communalism that has given to African Americans a means of survival in a hostile racial environment over the centuries.

In 1989 I was finally granted a visa for my first visit to South Africa. Since I had related to the *Sullivan Principles* on a consistent basis, this longing to go to South Africa had a substantial foundation. Upon my arrival in Johannesburg, several individuals who had been contacted by my South African colleagues met me at the airport. I was offered a cottage in a plush location by a theologian who sent his assistant to greet me. A pastor who met me offered to house me until I could locate my own place. A Baptist missionary superintendent was also there to welcome me. Like most leaders from the United States, I could have become a spokesperson over the national television network to say favorable things on behalf of the racist regime and to visit the famous animal park. However, my mission was clear. I wanted to visit black people and witness their real condition in that black slum called Soweto. I declined all offers and asked my missionary friend to take me to the hotel where I had a prior reservation.

Within a few days I had settled in with a family in Soweto for my month's stay in that country. As I moved about the country as both a minister and theologian, I made my home with a middle-class family. The wife was a teacher and the husband a community activist. They had two children, a son and a daughter.

Because Forkie, the husband, was a devout churchman, family man, and servant of the people, he taught me much about the culture of the people. The sense of the extended family and the oneness of community impressed me. This family had a well-built and comfortable home, but it was located in a real slum. There was little space between the houses. There was raw garbage in the streets. The roads were muddy and unpaved. When I asked my host how he was able to build such a comfortable house, he told me that his friends, especially in the church where he belonged, supplied both the materials and the labor to assist him in building his family home. We spent many hours in conversation after the family retired in the evening. He filled in the outline of the saying "Because I am we are; and because we are, I am." Forkie spelled out for me in concrete ways how the proverb continues to function in the sense of peoplehood in the most adverse circumstances, where a people exist on the edge of survival.

This experience in Soweto and other parts of the continent gave me a deep appreciation for both our African roots and our experiences in this country. I am a son of the South. I have known communities where a sense of family radiates throughout a small community. If there is illness or death and if there is a need for shelter or the adoption of children, the need is met collectively. Sometimes this takes place through a church, but it goes beyond the witness of any minister or congregation. The unchurched as well as believers share in providing for those in trouble or in need. In spite of our long separation from the motherland, we still need not only to remember but also to cultivate and celebrate such values of sharing and caring.

The leaders among blacks in the 1960s demonstrated this sense of togetherness, and we were pushed forward by their vision and sacrifices. The noblest example is Martin Luther King Jr., but many unsung heroes — men and women — lived by this creed. They sought to help the weak and the helpless.

We face a new mindset today among those who are called Buppies, middle-aged, middle-class blacks who have been successful according to American mainstream values. With their position, wealth, and popularity, they are lifted up as examples for the rest of black America. Though they have succeeded due to affirmative action, they are now against this project. They are individualistic in their outlook and lifestyle, no longer wanting to be associated with the underclass, even those in their own bloodline. They want to cut bait with their past. Their reward is often loneliness, even nihilism. Often they are rejected by the white Americans with whom they desire to associate, and they have burned the bridges to their past.

Recently two famous black athletes have been much in the national news: Sammy Sosa and Michael Jordan. Here in Durham, near Jordan's home, I have seen the great outpouring of praise for Jordan's greatness on the basketball court. The news accounts speak of his wealth and fame. There seems to be an obsession concerning this standard of success. Enough is enough! I begin to think about where Jordan came from and the underclass left behind. Many gifted boy athletes want to follow him but will never make it. Many of them have other talents and abilities that could lead them to make a great contribution to the human family, but there is not the glamour, fame, and wealth that is bestowed upon the black athlete or entertainer. Our youth need a sense of peoplehood, a larger vision of fulfillment for their lives, and the sense of community.

If we discover our Africentric roots we begin to celebrate our great heritage and join the community. We seek a better life together. Dr. Benjamin E. Mays often said: "The strength of the wolf is in the pack, and the strength of the pack is in the wolf." By this he meant that our strength as individuals is in our peoplehood and the strength of our people is in individuals.

While some powerful African American leaders are co-opted and separated from their people, others are in positions of influence but solidly anchored in the life of the black community. During the Martin Luther King Jr. celebration in January 1999 at Duke University, we were privileged to have two such persons. They are obviously in continuity with their African American heritage with African roots, but they also reach out to all people. Julian Bond, chair of the board of the National Association for the Advancement of Colored People (NAACP), and U.S. Surgeon General David Satcher are persons who can associate with the high and mighty but have not lost the common touch. As they speak you can follow them as they recall their roots, but they also address national and international concerns for all people. They seek to use their experience to bring people together with justice and equality. They do so while drinking deeply from the well of their Africentric roots.

In this chapter, I described the manner in which the Africentric perspective leads to greater self-esteem. This self-esteem has a personal and a communal dimension. Though I found it necessary to isolate the personal from the communal, they are usually present in the same persons. We are fulfilled when we are aware that we are persons in community. The Africentric perspective can bring enrichment and empowerment both to the person and to a people.

Notes

1. Charles H. Kraft, *Christianity and Culture* (Maryknoll, N.Y.: Orbis, 1979), 103–24.

2. Ibid., 107–8.

3. See Frederick C. Mish et al., eds., *Webster's Tenth Collegiate Dictionary* (Springfield, Mass.: Merriam-Webster, Inc., 1994).

4. Kraft, 111.

5. Ibid., 115.

6. Stokely Carmichael and Charles V. Hamilton, *Black Power* (New York: Vintage, 1967).

7. Gabriel M. Setiloane, "Confessing Christ Today," *Journal of Theology in Southern Africa* 11 (July 1973): 31.

8. J. Deotis Roberts, *Roots of a Black Future: Family and Church* (Philadelphia: Westminster, 1980). A more comprehensive discussion of ministry, a list of the various forms of ministry, and a discussion on the black church tradition may be found in my *Prophethood of Black Believers* (Louisville, Ky.: Westminster/John Knox, 1994).

Chapter 8

Africentric Worship

The preacher tells of days long ago and of people whose sufferings were like ours...what we have not dared feel in the presence of the Lords of the Land, we now feel in church...our eyes become absorbed in a vision...the preacher begins to punctuate his words with sharp rhythms, and we are lifted far beyond the boundaries of our daily lives...until drunk with our enchanted vision...we do not know who we are, what we are, where we are.... We go home pleasantly tired and sleep easily, for we know that we hold...a possibility of inexhaustible happiness.... We take this feeling with us each day and it drains the gall out of our years, sucks the sting from the rush of time, purges the pain from our memory of the past, and banishes the fear of loneliness and death.... Some say that, because we possess this faculty of keeping alive this spark of happiness under adversity, we are children. No for we know that there will come a day when we shall pour out our hearts over this land.

— RICHARD WRIGHT, *Twelve Million Voices*[1]

WE ARE INTRODUCED TO WORSHIP in the African American church through this quotation. Lest we misunderstand the nature of worship and its effects in the black church, we need to be reminded that the two ritual frames in African American worship are devotion and service. This doubleness of our worship experience is rooted in African initiation rites. Worshippers are transported psychically from a hostile and precarious world to a smaller and more secure one that will equip them to face that hostile environment again.[2] These two dimensions of black worship will be noted in the various aspects of Africentric worship to be discussed in this chapter.

Let us begin to look at Africentric worship. The worship began with powerful drumming. As the drummers moved toward the altar, a dozen dancers in colorful African attire followed them. The congregation was pleasantly surprised as the music and dancing reached a crescendo of praise. This experience of worship was unusual for this middle-class black church.

The choir, dressed in colorful African robes and kente cloth scarves, marched gleefully down the aisle toward the altar. The congregation, obviously transfixed by the cultural treat offered in the worship experience, joined with the choir in singing or humming the hymn of praise from Mother Africa. Even if they did not know the words, the tune seemed familiar.

This Africentric worship experience made full use of the African presence in music, dance, and spoken word. The display of African symbols, poetry, and drama by youthful leaders provided a climate of an African ancestral celebration that filled the sanctuary with a sense of pride of heritage.

The message conveyed in this moveable feast of music, drama, and spoken word was powerful. Not only did the people celebrate their heritage, but also this cultural expression through worship became a respectable medium that conveyed a sense of "somebodiness" throughout the congregation. The fellowship and common meal that followed demonstrated the potential of the Africentric perspective to enrich and empower African Americans in both devotion and service.

Worship is defined here in general terms, since it is found in all religions. It is adoration, homage, or veneration of a deity. There are rites, ceremonies, and prayers appropriate for adoration to a deity. It carries with it feelings of adoration directed to the being reverenced. In this chapter, I will discuss briefly the place of music and prayer in Africentric worship. Thereafter I will look at the contribution of other fine arts to enrich Africentric worship. The chapter will close with a summary of the benefits of Africentric worship.

Music: An Africentric Focus

Music is a powerful gift of African Americans in all settings, sacred and secular.[3] Wherever one finds people of African descent in worship, there is musical expression. Music sets the tone for meaningful worship in the black church. It is at the heart of worship, and musical selections are likely to be spread throughout the worship experience. The worship leader and the choir director plan carefully where and when the music is to be used in order to maximize its effects upon the assembly or worshippers. Music attracts youth and has a special power to generate intergenerational fellowship. Vigorous pastoral leadership is essential.

Music is a form of expression that bears cultural traits from generation to generation. Therefore, as we reclaim our heritage, we convey a powerful Africentric message through music. Much has been said about the oral tradition of African American people, in which music is a means by which we can and do communicate the message of "redemption and release" across the generations.

It is essential that we teach music appreciation classes in our church education programs. Our songs have deep roots in our heritage and say a lot about our personal and social experience decade by decade. Therefore, it is important for the young to know the set of circumstances that gave rise to a particular type of music. Black youth need to know the circumstances that gave rise to the spirituals, the blues, jazz, gospel, and rap. Even so-called secular forms of black music convey a bright and healing message. The Africentric perspective on music can greatly enhance the importance of black worship.

Africentric Prayer

"We know not what we should pray for as we ought: but the Spirit itself maketh intercession for us with groanings which cannot be uttered" (Romans 8:26).

In order to appreciate the prayer tradition and its impact on black worship, one should read two books on prayer in the black church tradition. First, the late professor James Melvin Washington has left us a collection of prayers covering more than 250 years that have been placed in their historic context. His *Conversations with God*[4] is a classic study of prayer in the African American church tradition. This should be read alongside Harold A. Carter's *The Prayer Tradition of Black People.*[5]

Carter resists the notion that prayer is a form of human resignation to one's conditions. Rather, it is "a source of inner release and personal fulfillment" that can fortify one's determination to seek a complete participation in the family and community.[6] The study and use of the prayers of the black church tradition put us in touch with the richness of our Africentric religious heritage. Carter observes that "the Black prayer tradition must be seriously rethought and consciously revived if this valuable source of traditional spiritual power is to serve the ongoing needs of the Black person in today's world."[7]

In an important chapter on the relation between prayer and social change, Carter provides illustrations of how African American activists throughout slavery and to the present have turned to prayer as a powerful means of liberation. Sojourner Truth, George Washington Carver, Martin Luther King Jr., and many others illustrate the meaning of prayer in the struggle for freedom as well as mere survival. He includes "The Negro National Anthem" of James Weldon Johnson as a model prayer. His reasons are as follows:

> This prayer...embraces the concerns and elicits the allegiance of the Black community, regardless of denominational affiliation or cultural status.... It gives profound credit to God for our past and our present, and it looks to God for our future. It faces the plight we have come through and calls on us to be vigilant against the "wine of the world."[8]

We close these reflections on prayer in the Africentric perspective by reminding the reader of Johnson's prayer, which concludes with a call to remain loyal to both our God and native Africa.[9]

Africentrism and the Fine Arts

Two forms of artistic expression deserve more attention in black worship: drama and dance. Often members of black churches attend religious dramas, plays presented to religious people from all racial and ethnic backgrounds. Nothing is wrong with this if the particular drama conveys a vital message. However, the drama usually is based upon a literal interpretation of Scripture and a one-sided view of salvation. The message is not very helpful for an oppressed group. There is no reason this same art form could not be used to convey a balanced view of salvation. It could also be placed in an Africentric context.

There is more involved than cultural difference. Many black plays are unsuitable for other reasons. Dramatists who have little regard for the black church and the gospel present them. The worship is presented as all emotion with little meaning. It is billed as entertainment without regard to the real nature and mission of the black church. The black church as an institution responsible for the salvation and survival of black people becomes an object of shame and disgrace.

We need more people with a knowledge of drama who will be able to present the black church properly, with respect. This will require persons who appreciate their African roots but who also have knowledge and commitment to the Christian faith.

As an assistant pastor at the Union Baptist Church of Hartford, Connecticut, many years ago, I encouraged a drama teacher, George Thomas, to attempt a dramatic presentation. Thomas, a member of Union Baptist, was also a high school teacher. In his role as a teacher he taught drama and directed plays. He agreed to direct a play at the church, and as minister to youth, I assisted him in the selection of the play and the recruitment of actors from among the youth in the church. Young people were excited about participation, and many adults agreed to assist us. It developed into a congregational project.

Several rehearsals included meals and fellowship. Those who worked together to stage the production grew spiritually as they got to know each other better. When it was presented the play drew a large audience from our congregation and other congregations in the city. The effects upon the young people and their parents were profound. The drama brought gave a vivid account of real-life situations and conveyed to all who attended a vital religious experience. This experience convinced me that drama may be used in local churches in an effective way, especially when culture and vital religion are combined.

At the conclusion of Alexs Pate's *Amistad,* Cinque, of the African Mende tribe, is tried for mutiny. However, at the end of the story, he is more victor than victim. He shares wisdom from his African ancestors, telling his accusers that the Mende believe that when trouble comes one should summon the spirits of the ancestors. They have never left, he affirms. The wisdom and strength they had will come to our aid. Those who heard him understood what he meant was this: who we are is who we were.[10] This is the Africentric outlook. Drama can help us convey this message in various forms, including worship in the African American church.

Like drama, dance is an art form that carries forth the essence of the African American cultural heritage in a powerful way.[11] Dance, both sacred and secular, is common as a cultural art form in Africultures worldwide. I have observed it in Brazil and Trinidad, in the United States, in Egypt, Togo, and Nigeria, and throughout other countries on the African continent, including South Africa. It is said that when slave masters and their preachers forbade converted slaves to dance they shouted. We are a people with rhythm in our very being, and dance is a way of expressing this rhythm. Thus we need to acquire a deeper knowledge of the nature and meaning of the dance tradition. It can enrich and empower our worship.

Kariamu Walsh Asante, in a helpful study on African dance, finds a commonality in African dances across Africa. Intrinsic to African dance is a unity through epic, memory, oral tradition, and ancestral connection. Dances represent differences in languages, peoples, geographies, and cultures. Yet African dance is polyrhythmic, polycentric, and holistic with regard to motion. Motion is more important than posture or position.

Kariamu Asante lists several elements that make up African dance. First is the sense of movement she calls polyrhythm. Second is polycentrism, movement or motion spending time. Third is the curvilinear type of motion, for the circle has a special place. In the African world there is power in the circle. Fourth is a sense of dimensionality. The dimensional aspect is characteristic of all the senses in that it is by definition extrasensory, involving the oral tradition. Instead of materialistic imitation, sensual imitation, such as the rhythm of waves or the whisper or thunder of an elephant's walk, is used. Fifth is the epic memory. A memory is called forth that delivers to the viewer the pathos, feeling, and experience without telling the literal story. There is a spiritual dimension to this concept of experience. The creation of the dance draws upon a spirituality and epic memory embedded in the work. Sixth is a holistic sense. For instance, silence or stillness is as much a part of the dance as music or sound or movement. If the silence is broken, the rhythm is broken and the meaning of the dance is destroyed. Seventh is repetition. The experience is intensified through repetition of one movement, one sequence, or the entire dance. Intensification is not static but goes by repetition from one level to another until ecstasy, euphoria, possession, saturation, and satisfaction have been reached.[12]

Traditional dancers are prepared to perform through a warm-up before performance time. This readies the dancers in African dance to "go on stage dancing." In order to understand the dance in the African perspective it is important to have a view of aesthetics in the African cultural context. However, dance offers a significant insight into African culture.[13] Now that we have before us an account of what is involved in the dance in Africentric perspective, we may take a look at the use of dance in a worship setting.

In late November 1998 a group of African American religious scholars visited the New Covenant Baptist Church in Orlando, Florida. The Reverend Randolph Bracey Jr. is pastor and founder. We witnessed a traditional worship service, with one awesome exception. A group of dancers opened the worship experience with a liturgical dance ceremony. It was well done and produced a meaningful Africentric climate for the evening worship. The dancers returned later to lift up the spirits of the worshippers. All other aspects of the evening, including a fellowship meal, were common in black churches, but the Africentric liturgical dancing made the worship at New Covenant Baptist Church memorable and special. This experience, and others like it, convinced me of the power, meaning, and place of the Africentric dance in black worship to inspire and heal the worshippers.

African American Preaching

African Americans' strong oral tradition of communication has African roots. The spoken word has a special place in an oral tradition. We have been blessed with a distinguished group of orators and preachers of the gospel. In this company have been many African American women. The preaching event is the centerpiece of black worship, especially in Protestant circles. As one who sometimes lectures in places where a sermon is expected, I will illustrate my point by an incident I encountered a few years ago.

I was asked to provide a lecture on the black family and church based upon my book *The Roots of a Black Future*. The Progressive Baptist Convention had invited me to lecture at the end of the morning seminar sessions and before lunch, a time customarily set aside for a sermon. I arrived a few minutes early and was seated in the front row of seats near the pulpit where I was to speak. Two women seated behind me were engaged in conversation. One said to the other: "I came here to hear some good preaching. I understand, however, that someone by the name of Roberts is going to give a lecture." The other woman strongly agreed with this comment.

It is an understatement to say that this conversation dampened my spirit. I had second thoughts about the lecture. Should I abandon my prepared text and preach, or should I stick to my assignment? I decided on a lecture sermon. I didn't, however, give up the content of my prepared text. I believed that the leadership had seen a need for what I had to say from my research and reflection. The discussion that followed and discussion over lunch justified my decision. Nevertheless, this event did remind me of the important place that preaching has in black worship. Many African Americans depend upon it for spiritual nurture.

Rev. Dr. Olin Moyd, pastor of the Mt. Lebanon Baptist Church of Baltimore, Maryland, has written an important book on preaching and theology in the African American church tradition, *The Sacred Art: Preaching and Theology in the African American Tradition.* Moyd reminds us that preaching is the centerpiece of worship in the black church. It brings black spirituality and the strong oral tradition of black folks together.

Phillips Brooks, a noted preacher, alluded to preaching as "the communication of truth through personality." This is a truism if one observes the effectiveness of outstanding black preachers. Early in my ministry, I was privileged to listen to renowned preachers, especially during my student days at Shaw University's Divinity School. Shaw University is a Baptist institution, and many of these notable preachers were Baptists. It is not merely the oratorical gifts of these preachers but also the freedom of expression and the affirmation of the people who place special emphasis upon sermon delivery.

The appreciation for effective sermon delivery is not limited to African Americans. In my doctoral study days in Edinburgh, Scotland, I found a similar appreciation for the sermon as the center of worship and a marked similarity between preaching in Scotland and preaching in African American churches.

Between 1955 and 1957, when I studied in Scotland, I already had considerable experience as pastor and preacher. However, the pulpit supply administrator in the Office of the Church of Scotland told me that I would not be well received by most congregations. I was soon to learn that this was only his personal point of view. I related this conversation to other leaders in the Church of Scotland, but they readily sent me to vacant pulpits. I was warmly received, and my preaching style was fully accepted.

Within the Church of Scotland were many outstanding preachers. These preachers had good content in their sermons, and they also preached with eloquence and passion. My favorites were Pastor Murdo McDonald of St. Georges West, Edinburgh, and Professor James Stewart, who taught on the Edinburgh Divinity Faculty in New Testament Studies and served as a chaplain to the queen. Thus I discovered that the gift of preaching is found in other cultures.

Among the present-day leading African American preachers are James Forbes of the Riverside Church of New York City; Dr. Gardner C. Taylor, pastor emeritus of Concord Baptist Church, Brooklyn, New York; Jeremiah A. Wright Jr. of the Trinity United Church of Christ, Chicago, Illinois; and Peter J. Gomes, Dean of Chapel at Harvard University. Jeremiah A. Wright Jr. is also a noted Africentric scholar. While these have been noted, I am aware of an abundance of effective preachers in the African American pulpits nationwide.

Freedom in the Baptist tradition may have aided the development of many effective preachers. Nevertheless, effective preaching is not limited to any one denomination in the African American church tradition. The black church is essentially pulpit-centered. Some African Americans, for example, Episcopalians and Roman Catholics, worship in altar-centered churches. But even in altar-centered churches, many pastors or priests began in the late 1960s and early 1970s to use the black preaching style. They found that black preaching upgraded attendance and membership. It created a warmer and friendlier fellowship, and it enhanced their outreach ministry, especially in the slums of major cities.

The black theology movement was thoroughly ecumenical. In the early stages of this movement, I was often called upon to be a retreat leader among black Catholics. My assignment was that of a theologian. I was pleasantly surprised that these religionists were seeking to recover their African roots. They used black sacred music (i.e., hymns and spirituals), and they were developing a black Mass. On several occasions I was asked to deliver a closing sermon. They were desirous of being in touch with the black preaching tradition. Here I refer to a style of preaching that has profound theological and biblical content. However, it also included the passion that goes into effective African American preaching.

W. Holmes Borders, one of the outstanding black preachers of his day and pastor of Wheatstreet Baptist Church in Atlanta, recalled an illustrative event. An unschooled mother who came out of the black Baptist church tradition accompanied her college-educated daughter to an Episcopal church. As the priest took the congregation through the liturgy, the mother became restless. As the ritual neared completion, the mother inquired, "When are we going to hear some preaching?" Her daughter said, "The priest has already delivered his homily." Responding honestly, the mother said, "I thought those were the announcements." Preaching in the black church tradition is an awesome event for both the preacher and the congregation. When it is missing, the African American worshipper feels a lack of a vital encounter with God.

I delivered two presentations at Eastern Baptist Theological Seminary in Philadelphia on February 15, 1999. During the morning I delivered the Frank Mitchell Lecture in the seminary chapel. In mid-afternoon, I preached for the Baptist Minister's Conference. Both events were in the same location. However, in the afternoon the rostrum became a pulpit. The afternoon audience was not academic but an assembly of fellow pastors and preachers. My task was not that of a theologian but that of a preacher of the gospel. I now stood behind the sacred desk. I felt the awesomeness of my task. At this time I knew that my task was more spiritual than intellectual. One is humbled by this assignment and one rightly inquires from God, What will you say through me to the people of God?

Africentric Preaching

African Americans may have any number of views regarding Africa. I hear ordinary, unlettered blacks glibly say, "I am an American, not African!" Some are well-educated African Americans who feel that they have outgrown any connection with Africa. The attitude of African Americans toward Africa may range from disinterest to Africentric celebration. This range of feelings is not associated with class. It reflects instead the inability to appreciate the importance of roots in affirming who we are as persons and as a people. Regardless of our station in life, our ancestral origin is in Africa. This is where we came from. We have more in common with our African kin than skin color. The source of our culture is African. To affirm our African roots does not mean a rejection of American fruit. We can be fully African American and hold a genuine Africentric perspective.

In view of the fact that our exposure to knowledge and culture has been Euro-American, we can readily understand the lack of knowledge and confusion African Americans show regarding their African background. We have been exposed to Greek mythology instead of Egyptian mythology. The same is true of philosophy and art. Even the study of the Bible, our textbook for preaching, has not taken into account the positive references to Africa, the land of Moses' birth, Israel's infancy, and Jesus' childhood. We have not been aware of the African connection as we have searched the Scriptures for preaching texts. Nevertheless, any standard Bible concordance reveals the names of great Africans such as Hagar, Abraham's wife; Ebed-melech, Jeremiah's Egyptian deliverer; Simeon, Jesus' cross-bearer; and Queen Candace's Nubian treasurer. Texts for preaching and teaching like these can inspire people to embrace Mother Africa. This may lead them to esteem their Africanness as a gift of God.[14]

Emil Thomas demonstrates his point by using words from Matthew 2:13: "The angel of the Lord appeareth to Joseph in a dream, saying, Arise, and take the young child and his mother, and flee into Egypt." The sermon topic is "The Drama of a Daddy with a Dream." This sermon is designed to lift the aspirations of black people and provide a sense of purpose, dignity, and destiny.[15] Black womanist theologians like Delores Williams have focused upon the story of Hagar. This use of Scripture has meant much to inspire black women to self-respect and to faith in God who "makes a way out of no way."[16]

Any preacher needs to be in touch with the people's experience. Karl Barth's statement that the preacher needs to have the Bible in one hand and the newspaper in the other bears much weight. The preacher needs to make contact with the people in their *Lebenswelt* (living world), which is why the pastor-preacher is more effective than an occasional preacher. I speak from experience, because I have been both a pastor-preacher and a full-time theologian who sometimes preaches. A preacher who lives among people as a spiritual director, counselor, and friend knows their joys and sorrows. When that pastor mounts the pulpit, he or she is aware of how the gospel may touch lives at a profound level. Preachers are charged with the responsibility of a divinely given challenge — to deliver a word from

God to the people. There is no greater earthly assignment than this. One should never deliver a sermon without the people's concerns in mind and without much study and prayer.

Years ago I had a field trip into several African countries. In Lagos, Nigeria, I attended a worship service in a large African congregation. The young pastor and preacher was educated in the United States. I paid special attend to his sermon content and delivery. During the other aspects of the worship, I had observed the responsiveness to music and prayers. I was very much at home. It reminded me of a typical black urban congregation in the United States. The responses were similar. The preacher began by using his scholarly exegesis of Scripture and his Western illustrations. The audience was silent and unresponsive. Suddenly the preacher became more passionate in his preaching. His illustration came out of his boyhood in an African village. At this point the people vocally responded to the preacher as they affirmed the manner in which his message made contact with their own experience. It was obvious that his message now came home to them in their context. His delivery was most effective in that African setting.

There is a cultural context that the preacher should know. This requires sensitivity as well as serious reflection. The preacher should be aware of what plumbs the emotional and volitional depths of the consciousness of parishioners. There is a need to know the history of the suffering as well as the immediate experiences of joy and sorrow. The Africentric elements in their experience are vital to the effective communication of a message of healing, deliverance, survival, and hope.

African American Christians love the Bible. Indeed, the love for the Bible is found broadly in our communities among the unchurched and unbelievers. The preachers must be acquainted with this sacred text. It helps to be a serious student of the Bible, its languages, textual analysis, history, and contexts. Interpreting the Bible is far more than reading it annually from cover to cover or memorizing texts. The Bible is a complex book — it is more like a library than one book. However, one must remember that it is an inspired book. God is speaking words of redemption through its pages.

The awesome task of the preacher is to proclaim the words of redemption to a people in need to face joys and sorrows, illness, and death. Black preaching at its best has made a great impact upon the lives of individuals and groups in the African American community in the past. If it is done well, it will continue to do so into the indefinite future. Effective Africentric preaching does not languish in cultural captivity. It is effective where there is found the human condition. Its anchor, however, is deeply embedded in black history and culture — in its Africentric roots.

Rites of Passage

Anthropologists use the rites-of-passage terminology in order to describe significant events in the life cycle of individuals and groups. Rites and ceremonies mark such events as birth, adulthood, marriage, and death. Let us consider two rites of passage — namely, the passage from childhood to adulthood and the wedding ceremony — from an Africentric perspective. We briefly describe the meaning of each and suggest the worship aspect in each case.

In every known culture is a socialization process that follows the development of children to adulthood. This explains the common beliefs and behaviors of individuals and groups in their living world. This socializing process is comprehensive in the African setting. Molefi Kete Asante notes how it began in the naming ceremony in ancient Africa (Nubia and Egypt):

> Thousands of years ago, every boy and every girl was given a name according to significance. A boy, for example, had to learn how to do certain things, would be initiated into the religion of the ancestors and certain professions. A girl, for example, would master knowledge of agriculture and the behavior of children. This means that information from family tradition would have been passed to children.[17]

The naming ceremony is important because it assists us in identifying who we are and where we think we should be going. Each time parents name a child they are saying something about the way they want the child to be, about how they see themselves, and about what the future of African people should be. That is to say, the name goes with the child as a symbol of the people.[18]

This brief reference to naming and its importance introduces us to the outlook of Africans in regards to rites of passage. We turn now to the initiation of boys into manhood. I have selected this rite for obvious reasons. I have in mind the crisis in the African American male population.

During the spring semester of 1999, I taught a course on Saturdays at Shaw University Divinity School. As I left the campus for return to Durham, I passed a rundown house where I saw a large number of black males, from five or six to about twenty-five years old, hanging out. This appears to be a male ritual. The boys, some of whom had attended school, joined older males who perhaps had been at this location daily. Some were no doubt unemployed and unemployable. Some also had been in prison and were sharing with the boys their experience behind bars. The boys, of tender years, viewed the situation as their destiny.

This scene can be duplicated nationwide as the plight of many black males who are moving from boyhood to manhood. So many are fatherless and without a responsible male role model that some form of incarceration is a self-fulfilling prophecy. Unless there is powerful personal intervention the future is bleak for many of our African American males.

Many years ago, I was born and reared on Prison Camp Road, near the foot of the mountains of North Carolina in a town known as Spindale. Due to the encouragement of parents, teachers, and ministers, I left home for college at the tender age of sixteen. As I look back over the years, I now am fully aware of the importance of this decision. Many of my male schoolmates were already in prison or the cemetery due to violence in this town.

Too often the circumstances of life prepare the way for a tragic future. Those in charge of the prison system often place the prison in the center of the African American community. There is a major city where I made a visit like this. A prison for hardcore criminals was located in a heavily populated location in the slums. Boys conversed with their older brothers, cousins, and sometimes fathers and uncles from prison bars. How tragic! To those boys the prison system was equated with manhood.

The prison system is only one threat. We also need to consider the drug culture. As we move into a highly skilled and technological culture, the lucrative underground economy of the drug market is extremely attractive. It is not too difficult to find raw recruits for drug dealing among young black males who see drug dealing as an easy way to economic success. They are lured into this trade by circumstances that seem to entrap them. Too often their adult role models are among their kin. The problem for many church and community leaders is not a lack of concern but of knowing what to do and how to do it.

The rite of passage from boys to men is critical at this point. I suggest two steps with an Africentric outlook. The first steps should be informational. If churches adopt the extended family model, a weekend male retreat is a possibility. An athletic activity may be included to attract boys to join the responsible adult males. However, once they are gathered there should be a culture- and Bible-based study of what it means to become an adult male. It is important that a growing boy meet and become acquainted with a responsible male role model. The role model should share aspects of his own life and how he was able to choose a worthy goal for his life and the influences that enabled him to overcome.

The boys should be asked to relate their daily experiences as black males and indicate what it is like to confront the distractions and temptations on the streets as they go from home to school and return home. The men present should be willing to adopt one or two boys and become big brothers in order to help socialize fatherless boys into responsible manhood.

The second step should involve a ceremony, "a worship experience," that would mark the passage from boyhood into manhood. Both stages are important: the informational, study, and retreat activities together with the association with a responsible Christian adult should prepare the way for the ceremony that is to mark the decision of the boy to accept the challenge of adulthood in the family, the church, and the community.

In the transition from childhood to adulthood, values and faith in God will need to be linked. It is one thing to know what one ought to do. It is another thing to find the will and resources of grace to reach one's goals. Africentric leaders need to work on both fronts. The testimony of those who have excelled in their efforts supports this view. They have come to themselves, sometimes as a prodigal son in the far country. It has, however, been their discovery of meaning through faith in God that has set them on a new path. Thus a good dose of cultural values should be supplemented by a profound faith to the ends we have in view.

At the appropriate time there should be a major ceremony in which the church community comes together and blesses and encourages these young men who have prepared themselves to face a responsible manhood.[19]

Barbara Eklof indicates that in planning a rites-of-passage celebration, one should keep in mind four primary goals: "celebrating the positive aspects of moving from childhood to adulthood; exalting our ancestral traditions; instilling a sense of values in the initiates while glorifying their physical, emotional, mental, spiritual uniqueness and creating an enthusiastic ceremonial atmosphere."[20] In addition she emphasizes "the Seven Principles of Blackness" established by Maulana Ron-Karenga discussed in chapter 6. Obviously these values are important for both women and men. An appropriate program should also be outlined for females. The ceremony should be undergirded by an adequate devotional experience. Africentric worship should be the context.

The Manhood Anointing Ceremony should take place when boys are between fourteen and eighteen years of age. The ceremony might follow this model:

> The male honoree lies face down on the floor before his parents. The mother says, "Arise, precious fruit of my womb and take my blessing."
> The honoree rises.
> The mother offers the first half of the anointing prayer, and the father completes it. Then the anointing begins. First, the father dips his thumb in the blessed oil or ointment and makes a triangle on his son's forehead. Then the mother dips her thumb in the same oil or ointment and makes a circle around the triangle.
> Your son is then spiritually anointed.
> The ceremony is concluded by an elder, minister or priest by these words: "Arise, precious fruit of our people and take my blessing."[21]

Food and communal fellowship will conclude the celebration.

Special Occasions: Family Reunions

Since the publication of Alex Haley's *Roots* and the public acclaim it received, African Americans have been in quest of their African roots. Long before *Roots*, however, attention had been given to bringing families together — ever since slavery, a system that dealt a destructive blow to black families. This was especially unfortunate since African Americans had come from a high regard for the extended family in Africa. Since whites did not regard blacks as humans, black families were divided up for pleasure and profit.

The Africentric cultural perspective should build upon the family reunion movement now in vogue. Churches and Christian leaders, lay and clerical, need to make sure that a proper religious focus is provided for the family reunion movement. During the several years that I have participated in representative annual family reunions, I have observed the social and religious potential of the movement.

The family reunion movement cultivates pride of heritage. It brings persons in an extended family network together in times of joy as well as sorrow. Many family members who are lonely and alienated in an indifferent secular society travel long distances to be with their loved ones. It is an intergenerational gathering. Young people get to meet a number of the members of the older generation who become role models. They also have an opportunity to meet kinfolk of their own generation, which enables them to grow up together. I have noted a caring and sharing spirit that spills over into ongoing relationships between cousins in the extended family. All the positive results of the reunion movement cannot be enumerated here.

We cannot take this movement for granted, and we are grateful for it. It has brought great benefits to black family life. However, it seems to me that churches have not become sufficiently involved in this movement to provide spiritual nurture and direction.

Fortunately, there is usually a ceremony. Nevertheless, it is often merely cultural and historical and does not inject much spiritual direction. What a wonderful opportunity to emphasize the place of the black family in the life of the church family! It is not sufficient to have the family to worship together in the usual way. Worship ought to be planned around the ministry to family. The Africentric perspective should be used to bring the proper emphasis to the richness of the African roots in our family life. The prayers, the music, the sermon, and liturgy should be suitable for the occasion. Food and fellowship should follow this ceremonial event.

In addressing the "occasion," Cheryl A. Kirk-Duggan makes this worthy observation:

We champion the spirit that has let us take a family, friends, and neighbors' children without state action. We celebrate the unity that let our mothers and their mothers come together and make warm quilts out of rags and old clothes. We thank God for fathers and mothers who sacrificed for us, who held down many jobs to feed us, educate us in the Lord, and who survived.[22]

According to this author, the prayer, the litany and a vow of commitment should follow. Her suggested litany closes with this meaningful statement "Praise God for all expressions of healthy, loving families. In thanksgiving, as we stand on the brink of this new day, on the horizon of hope...let the bonds honored here transcend time in the love of Christ Jesus."[23] The worship is to be set in a historical cultural context that is Africentric. The colors of African liberation — red and green — and some reflective poetry are to be used. Insofar as possible young people should be encouraged to use their talents in enriching the celebration.

Conclusion

An Africentric outlook may enrich and empower worship within black churches. We must maximize the involvement of more persons with special gifts and talents in the fine arts in our worship experiences. Many forms of music can be used. Young people learning to play various musical instruments should be able to exercise their talents in worship. Beyond music, dance and drama offer unusual opportunities for a significant number of church members to get involved in the enrichment and expansion of worship. By tapping into the rich cultural heritage of African Americans, an abundance of talents can be put to use to enrich and empower worship. The Africentric perspective on preaching, the rites of passage (initiation of youth into adulthood and weddings), and the family reunion can also enrich and empower these events in the experience of worship and lifestyle.

Notes

1. Quoted by Walter F. Pitts Jr. in *Old Ship of Zion* (New York: Oxford University Press, 1993), front page.

2. Comments by Vincent L. Wimbush, ibid., foreword, xv.

3. J. Deotis Roberts, *Prophethood of Black Believers* (Louisville, Ky.: Westminster/John Knox, 1994), chap. 10.

4. James Melvin Washington, *Conversations with God* (New York: HarperCollins Publishers, Inc., 1994).

5. Harold A. Carter, *The Prayer Tradition of Black People* (Valley Forge, Pa.: Judson, 1976).

6. Ibid., 20–21.

7. Ibid., 21.

8. Ibid., 115.

9. For a scholarly discussion on prayer by a historian of religion, see Friedrich Heiler, *Prayer: A Study in the History and Psychology of Religion*, trans. Samuel McComb and J. Edgar Park (New York: Oxford University Press, 1958), 4:356–57, 358, 361–63.

10. Alexs D. Pate, *Amistad: A Novel*, based on screenplay by David Franzoni and Steven Zaillian (New York: Dream Works, 1997), 298–99.

11. See Cecelia Williams Bryant, *I Dance with God* (Dallas, Tex.: Akosua Visions, 1995). In addition to reading that text, I have had the privilege of viewing the author (together with one of her daughters) present this message in the context of black worship. It is a superb rendition of Africentric worship through liturgical dancing.

12. Molefi Kete Asante and Kariamu Walsh Asante, *African Culture: The Rhythms of Unity* (Trenton, N.J.: African World Press, 1993), 71.

13. Ibid.

14. Henry Mitchell and Emil Thomas, *Preaching for Black Self-Esteem* (Nashville: Abingdon, 1994), 77–78.

15. Ibid., 77–86.

16. Delores Williams, *Sisters in the Wilderness* (Maryknoll, N.Y.: Orbis Books, 1994), chapter 1, 15–29.

17. Molefi Kete Asante, *The Book of African Names* (Trenton, N.J.: Africa World Press, 1982), 11.

18. Ibid., 9.

19. J. Garrot Benjamin Jr., *Boys to Men: A Handbook for Survival* (Indianapolis: Heaven on Earth Publishing House, 1993), 32.

20. Barbara Eklof, *For Every Season* (New York: HarperCollins, 1997), 144–45.

21. Ibid., 143. Cf. Paul Hill Jr., *Coming of Age* (Chicago: African American Images, 1992).

22. Cheryl A. Kirk-Duggan, *African American Special Days* (Nashville: Abingdon, 1996), 33–34.

23. Ibid., 37.

Chapter 9

Africentrism and Social Witness

THE TEST OF THE AFRICENTRIC PERSPECTIVE in the life of individuals and groups will be manifest in its effectiveness toward positive social change. What difference does Africentrism make in the personal and communal transformation of lifestyle? Will it help us engage the real issues? Will it help us solve any of the massive social ills that confront black people?

In this chapter I will make suggestions about the Africentric perspective concerning an outreach ministry, more details of which can be found in my *Prophethood of Black Believers*.[1] Here I have selected two examples of the manner in which an Africentric perspective can become functional in the witness of black churches: drug addiction and family life ministry. It is expected that the connection between the Africentric and effective church work in the black community is now apparent from this study. I will conclude this study with a concern for how one affirms an Africentric ministry of reconciliation with other racial and ethnic groups.

So many ills beset African Americans. We think of the curse of the drug culture, the scourge of AIDS, the warehousing of black males in prisons, absent black fathers, and the child mothers of black babies. The convergence of racism and poverty is bringing a trail of devastation to the black family and community. Our churches face an awesome challenge but at the same time an opportunity to make a difference in the lives of many people. This discussion assumes that understanding and using the Africentric perspective in our Christian witness can make a difference.

In late November 1997 I met Pastor Cecil Williams, who has declared war on the new slavery of drug addiction. His work in San

111

Francisco began in a street ministry on the corner of Ellis and Taylor streets, the location of Glide Memorial United Methodist Church. Over a three-day weekend, I was deeply impressed by several events I witnessed at that church. As Williams observes:

> I thought I had seen it all, but in the late 1980s, something toxic and lethal settled on the street. I began to smell death. The Tenderloin neighborhood looked the same. Flophouses, dealers, pimps, and refuse of humanity line the streets — nothing new about that. . . . But it wasn't the spiraling crime rate that smelled so bad; something else was stinking up the neighborhood. . . . I began to see women, many young mothers, strung out on crack cocaine, straggling through Boeddekar Park. They'd pull along their little children who were so dispirited they didn't even want to play. . . . The mothers were holding the hands of their children as they all meandered down a path of despair. Crack cocaine was causing the stench of death.[2]

"The smell of death . . . permeated [even] the neighborhoods of plenty,"[3] and Williams goes on to describe how corporate leaders, police, visitors, and fellow ministers viewed this situation. At a conference on this problem in Washington called by William Bennett of the Bush administration, Williams learned that the ready-made program called for more money for jails, cops, and guns. He knew that this program would put behind bars more children of poor black communities already burdened by the burden of despair. At the same time children from affluent neighborhoods would find a way to buy their freedom. Williams asserted: "They wanted our children. They wanted to imprison our future."[4]

In 1989 Williams organized his own national conference on the problem. Eleven hundred people attended this meeting, designated "The Death of a Race: The Black Family/Community and Crack Cocaine National Conference," at the Hilton across Taylor Street from his church. "All of those gathered stood up together. The Glide staff, black community leaders, addicts, prostitutes, grandmothers, poor and wealthy, illiterate and educated — we told our stories of faith and our stories of resistance."[5] The focus of this conference was a war on addiction, and it is to be noted that Cecil Williams believes that we live in a society of addicts. He writes: "When you become obsessed with anything to the extent that you rely on it for your grasp of reality, you are addicted."[6] In this he includes drugs, alcohol, cigarettes, food and even religion. We could easily add addictive gambling and sex.

At Glide Church

In Williams's church the recovery program is comprehensive and includes many outreach ministries. "People fan out throughout the building to recovery meetings, crisis care, social services, counseling, support groups, job training, computer classes, drug and pregnancy testing, HIV/AIDS information, child care, and church information."[7]

The Glide ministry is focused upon African Americans, who represent most of the crack addicts in Williams's ministry. Thus he seeks to make contact with cultural patterns in that community. He has found that the twelve-step approach of Alcoholics Anonymous is not effective or culturally appropriate for blacks; it is too individualistic. Blacks need to belong to an extended family and to a community. We must acknowledge our need for one another. Blacks in the San Francisco ghetto, many of whom have no everyday lives and are homeless, jobless, and have no reputations to protect, do not need to remain faceless and hidden in society. We are storytellers, an oral people who need to pass on our life histories through stories. We need to proclaim, "This is the truth about my life. My secrets and my addiction no longer have power over me. I am free." As the people told their stories in public and moved through a Four Steps program, recovery began. The steps are recognition, self-definition, rebirth, and community.[8]

Sunday morning worship at Glide included a powerful music presentation, but the pattern of worship was informal. People sat or stood wherever there was space. Children sat on the edge of the pulpit. Young people played an important part in worship. Street people testified concerning how they had recovered from drug addiction. Mothers were off drugs and attending to their children. Men had been released from prison and told their stories. The pastor's sermon centered around how faith had reclaimed lives from unimaginable depths of sin and shame. We experienced a moveable feast of stories of the miracle of grace. In addition, however, this church had follow-up activities throughout the week. The worship experience was really a celebration of the church's ongoing ministry to its members and the community made up of people of all backgrounds.

Africentric Perspectives on Family

We constantly hear conservative Christians and politicians speak of the need for family values. All persons concerned about stronger families and the values for the next generation stress this need. African Americans seek family values in relation to their faith commitment. Wade W. Nobles, a black social scientist, has provided an important perspective on the study of black family life. He observes that "Black Culture" is based on "an African world-view, and, therefore, we have a special way of viewing our own awareness of reality. This outlook must be defined by a particular group of people for themselves. It is deceptive to view the black family by norms imposed upon it from white families."[9]

In several publications, I have attempted to relate family to church and provide some biblical and theological perspectives on this subject matter, grasping it from the African point of view.[10] I have discussed the extended family as a model for family life. This form of organization is not unique to the African style — no one who has traveled in Asia, especially in India or in the Chinese territories, would make this claim. However, it does exist in Africa and in the African diaspora, including the United States, most prevalently among African Americans in the South. The extended family is also found among African Americans nationwide where this tradition has continued through migration or cultivation. This form of family organization often is expressed in the churches where such families are members.

In a small town in North Carolina, one large extended black family makes up much of the black population. The members of this family are generally educated or skilled. They are homeowners and enjoy a comfortable lifestyle. They are also members of the same church. In fact, these family members are among the pillars of that small congregation. It does not seem to matter that the church is Methodist. Most persons who marry into this extended family join this fellowship, become active members, and rear their children in this religious context. This family has an annual reunion, usually in this town, for family members nationwide. These family members return to this community from all over the nation.

The extended family perpetuates certain traditions, cultivates important cultural, ethical, and religious values, and transmits them to young people in the new generation. The local church has a central place in the life of young and old. This wholesome family organization, with its annual fellowship, means much for the socialization of the young. The youth in this family have been unusually free from drug addiction. Even the young males have drawn nurture from this extended family and are mostly responsible in their personal and family life, wherever they live.

One of the uncles who entered this family by marriage conversed with a nephew who lives in a city, away from his place of birth. During Thanksgiving the uncle visited at the nephew's home and observed many of the family values evident in the relation of the nephew to his wife and children. He was pleasantly surprised to have the nephew respond that he was indebted "to what you as a member of the family taught me." Furthermore, the nephew recalled the several visits he made during his boyhood and how the observations he made during those developmental years had helped him select the values he now lived by. Examples like this make one aware of the meaning of the African proverb "It takes a whole village to raise a child." In the Africentric perspective, the church may also function as an extended family.

During my early ministry, I was privileged to serve as an assistant pastor in the Union Baptist Church in Hartford, Connecticut. In that congregation and throughout the black church community, I was able to observe how blacks had combined the extended family model with church participation and organization. Within my congregation were clusters of people from North Carolina, Georgia, South Carolina, Virginia, and Florida. Many of these people knew each other before they came North. It was more obvious in social events such as cookouts than in the fellowship encounters in church assemblies, but the extended family model existed in the churches in the same manner. On the other side of the account were congregations where the membership consisted primarily of persons from a Southern state. These congregations often called a pastor from the state from which its membership had migrated. The pastor was in a sense the chief parent of a family. In this way the extended family model with African roots that had been sustained through the tragic experience of slavery was evident in the church life of blacks in the North.

It is one thing to observe this cultural trait as a social scientist and another to observe it as a minister. One begins to seek many creative possibilities to turn this extended family pattern into a means for outreach, witness, and service. It can, if left to itself, degenerate into division and conflict. If, however, on the more programmatic front one turns this extended family pattern into a basis for ministry, the church as a whole can be seen as a sharing and caring fellowship. This cultural trait can become a vehicle of God's redeeming grace for witness and service. As the family of God the church embraces all individual families in God's household where God the divine Parent redeems and nurtures us all.

Notes

1. J. Deotis Roberts, *The Prophethood of Black Believers: A Political Theology for Ministry* (Philadelphia: Westminster/John Knox, 1994).

2. Cecil Williams, *No Hiding Place* (San Francisco: HarperCollins, 1992), 2.

3. Ibid., 3.

4. Ibid., 4.

5. Ibid., 5.

6. Ibid., 7.

7. Ibid., 6.

8. Ibid., 9. The process is described on 9–12.

9. Wade W. Nobles, *Africanity and the Black Family* (Oakland, Calif.: A Black Family Institute Publication, 1985), 64–65.

10. See J. Deotis Roberts, *Roots of a Black Future* (Philadelphia: Westminster, 1980).

Chapter 10

Africentrism and Multiculturalism

THE TERMS "Africentrism" and "multiculturalism" are very much in vogue,[1] and the relation between these two perspectives must be addressed theologically.

Demonstrating a concern to improve race relations and to support diversity, President Clinton made a strong statement on diversity in his State of the Union speech of 1998. However, African Americans need to approach multiculturalism with caution. Diversity, like love, can cover a multitude of sins. At the same time that we celebrate diversity, we have an alarming report of the plight of black Americans in 1998. A comparative study of the present status of blacks as compared with the Kerner Commission report, at least two decades ago, indicates that conditions are not as rosy as they seem. The report from the Milton S. Eisenhower Foundation indicates that the divide between the races has expanded: "The economic and racial divide in the United States not only has materialized, it's getting wider."[2]

Fred Harris, a member of the Kerner Commission that spoke of two societies, one black and the other white, once observed: "People need to become aware that things are getting worse again. . . . They need to see their own self-interest in this—that it doesn't make sense to have these under-utilized regions in the country and the under-utilized people whose lives are being wasted."[3] The report provides statistical evidence that should disturb all United States citizens:

While the national jobless rate is below 5 percent, unemployment rates of young men in places like south-central Los Angeles have topped 30 percent. The child poverty rate in the United States is four times the average of [that in] Western European countries, the incarceration rate of black men in the United States is four times higher than the same

117

rate in South Africa under apartheid, and 43 percent of minority children attend urban schools, usually where more than half the students are poor and more than two-thirds fail to reach even basic levels of national tests.[4]

This report, broader than the Kerner report, emphasizes minorities and the poor and reflects awareness of the growing diversity of the underclass in the United States. While a small group of Americans are becoming enormously wealthy, the underclass is growing. This is being fueled by the influx of large numbers in nonwhite peoples from all over the world, especially from the Southern Hemisphere.

While African Americans represent just one of the groups in the mix of ethnic groups, they have been in the United States for a long time and have helped build this nation with centuries of free and underpaid labor. They have suffered indignities and injustices, and they have shed their blood in the interest of our country. They have not only an experience of oppression over a long period of time but also hindsight about racism and ethnic cleansing that many nonwhite newcomers do not have. We African Americans must be clear on the distinction between issues of diversity or multiculturalism. Our struggle to be free as a people must continue. At the same time, we should be the first group to support other ethnic groups seeking to be free and equal in our society. The issues are illustrated for me in the Asante-Schlesinger conversation.

Political Unity versus Cultural Reality

Asante's critique of Arthur M. Schlesinger's *The Disuniting of America* is perceptive. He notes that Schlesinger's distinction between political unity and the United States cultural reality helps me to see more clearly the meaning of multiculturalism. Asante's defense of Africentrism helps to clarify his understanding of the movement he heads and the place of Africentrism in the context of cultural diversity or multiculturalism.

Schlesinger expresses his concern for the negative impact of Africentrism upon "America's core identity." His view of the United States is based upon the domination of Anglo-Saxon whites as a norm for the society. White culture thus defined represents the example to which others are expected to aspire. This vision of our society is psychologically edifying. It justifies the domination of European culture in America over all other cultures. This, from a cultural perspective, is the America of the past. It does not describe the country we now live in. This vision of America presented by Schlesinger, if put into practice, would be a most divisive factor at the present time with so many cultures present in the United States.

Africentrism, as defined by Asante, does not require that others deny their cultures but that African Americans join others on equal terms. Asante's views on Africentrism are clearly inclusive — not anti-white but pro-African in the context of cultural diversity.

> The person who believes that the African-American must be recentered, relocated in terms of historical referent, is not anti-American. . . . It suggests the strengths of this country compared to other countries. The conviction that we will defend the rights of all cultural expressions, not just Greco-Roman-Hebraic-Germanic-Viking cultures, must be strongly embedded in our political psyches if this Nation is to survive.[5]

In Asante's view American society is not static but dynamic, so we must constantly reinvent ourselves in light of our diverse experiences. "Try to make African and Asian copies of Europeans and women copies of men and you will force the disunity Schlesinger fears."[6] According to Asante, "the unity of America is based upon shared goals, a collective sense of mission, a common purpose and mutual respect."[7] Multiculturalism requires a multicultural curriculum, a multicultural approach to institutional building, and so forth. Africentrists say, according to Asante, that one should not be able to declare competency in music, for example, without having been introduced to spirituals, Duke Ellington, or the blues.[8] As a student in a black college, I was introduced to classical European music as well as black music, and the benefit of this experience has lasted for a lifetime. I am able to appreciate all musical events — Japanese, Indian, or African music, and not black music only. Similarly we must prepare our youth, cross-culturally, to participate fully in a multicultural society.

Thus, concerning the unity of American, I agree with Asante that the United States is a diversity without ethnic or cultural hegemony. We have many cultures interacting with each other, but only one society. Therefore it is no longer viable for white cultures to parade as the only American culture.[9]

Africentrists begin all education by starting all analysis from the African person as agent. This means that the African American child must be connected, grounded in the same way that white children are grounded, when we discuss literature, history, mathematics, and science. Asante remarks: "Africentrists do not take anything away from white history except its aggressive urge to pose as universal."[10]

The real question is whether Eurocentrism can exist without the denial of the other. "We ought, therefore, to be able to develop a curriculum of instruction that affirms all people in their cultural heritages."[11] It is unfortunate that many Euro-Americans identify nationality with culture. One's citizenship can be American while his or her historical and cultural origins are African, Latino, Asian, Native American, or European.

Finally, Asante makes a point that I believe needs to be taken with all seriousness. As a reference to political unity rather than cultural diversity, the phrase *E pluribus unum* makes a lot of political sense. Originally it referred to several colonies dovetailing into one federal government. Thus we have many states but one central government. The reference is to our political structure, but we need another statement about the American cultural reality. Instead of multiculturalism threatening the unity of America, it faces our real cultural condition. It is the way forward for our great nation. Asante concluded this discussion with Schlesinger on a powerful note: "What we can wish for and realize is a society of mutual respect, dynamism, and decency. Rather than labeling or setting cultural groups against each other, we should empower a vision that sees the American Kaleidoscope of cultures as uniquely fortunate."[12]

Looking at multiculturalism from the Africentric point of view, Asante has come up with a more operable paradigm than one usually applied to cultural relations in our society. His paradigm seems dynamic and operable and provides an excellent context for affirming both the Africentric perspectives and multiculturalism.[13]

Multiculturalism/Africentrism and Future Shock

Future Shock, Third Value, and *Power Shift,* all by Alvin Toffler, have become best-sellers because they say something about ourselves that we feel deeply but have not clearly understood. A comment about

Power Shift in *The New York Times Book Review* is representative of the appraisal of this book: "By placing the accelerated changes of our current information age in the larger perspective of history, Mr. Toffler helps us to face the future with less wariness and more understanding." This is necessary for all people. However, it is more compelling for an oppressed people to constantly assess what is happening to them at each period in history. We need self-understanding, and we need people understanding at each period of time. What does it mean for us to stand in the last decade of the twentieth century and anticipate the twenty-first century?

A West Indian friend who is trying to understand what it means to be black in the United States recently observed that the "Africentric" idea may last only a few years and then we will see something else. My immediate response was that might well be, but it will be circumstances that force an ideological shift. The constant for us, I said, is *freedom!* We may shift tactics and strategies, but our eyes are stayed on freedom. Look at the terms that have been used for self-definition in the last fifty years. We have been Negro, colored, Afro-American, black, and African American. In some cases the terms have been given to us, and in others we have coined them. But we have in all cases accepted their usage for self-reference. Each term points to a period in the life of black people in the United States in their quest for freedom for themselves and their children. The terms under consideration should be seen as having profound meaning at the present. It does not matter how long they will be in vogue as long as they lead us forward toward the freedom and dignity of persons.

Another word needs to be said. Our suffering as a people is intergenerational. Therefore, there is continuity as well as discontinuity in the usage of terms for self-definition. For instance, there is a continuity between blackness and Africentricity. Asante builds upon the legacy of the black power/black consciousness movement. Malcolm X is, for him, a hero of the struggle for freedom.

What does "African American" mean? In my understanding, it includes the best understanding of black power and consciousness. However, it meets certain needs that have arisen in the situation due to cultural diversity in the United States population. The number of nonwhite immigrants in this country is increasing. The birthrate among the nonwhite population is also very high. While the percentage of white people in this country is decreasing due to less immigration and low birthrates, the percentage of nonwhites is increasing at a rapid rate. At the dawn of the twenty-first century, the United States is moving toward a nonwhite majority.

Because of this development, African Americans will be part of a cultural diversity in the United States that differs from that of the past. Though sharing many cultural and color similarities with the newcomers, African Americans are a unique group of people, having been in the United States more than three centuries. We cannot escape this history of oppression — what it has done against us as well as what it has done for us. We are a talented people who have made a great contribution to this nation in spite of or because of our harsh experiences. We cannot gainsay the fact that we have also shared in the progress of this nation.

What determines the meaning of "African American" is how we understand ourselves and how we see our relationship with others in the diverse cultural society. It can be significant to call ourselves African Americans if we do not take difference to mean deficiency. Furthermore, it is important that we claim the parity of our rich culture and insist upon the right to affirm it alongside all other cultures in the mix.

Multiculturalism is not pluralism. In my view, pluralism takes Euro-American culture to be normative. All other cultures are expected to measure their worth by conformity to that norm. If multiculturalism recognizes the diversity of cultures and at the same time allows each cultural group to appreciate the richness inherent in itself, then we can be Africentric and at the same time be equal participants in a multicultural society. Our worldview can be Africentric without looking either up or down at other cultures. Eurocentrism operates in theology. For example, who defines "evangelical"? This term does not seem to mean the same in the experience of black and white Christians.

"African American," properly understood, is not inconsistent with Africentricity on the one hand and multiculturalism on the other. It means that we can be African-centered while others may be European-centered and stand as equal partners with each and all. We can lay claim to self-esteem and pride of heritage because we are invested with our noble classical roots. We no longer define ourselves by slavery and victimization due to racial bias. We were somebody as a people many thousands of years in the era before Christ. Once we claim Egypt and Ethiopia as part of our heritage as an African people, it enhances and empowers us for the present and the future. We no longer see ourselves as former slaves only.

Leon Sullivan recalls an incident in his childhood in West Virginia. As a teenager, he went into a drugstore, sat down at the counter, and ordered some ice cream. The manager refused to serve him, saying, "Boy, get up on your feet and get out of here!" Sullivan recalls this was a summons to him. He took it as a challenge to "get up, stand up," and he has never bowed down. We are aware of his unusual contribution to economic development through Opportunities Industrialization Centers (OICs) and the black churches. He is now also engaged in educational and agricultural development work in Africa. In his own way, he has entered into a pragmatic economic form of Pan-Africanism.

Sullivan's experience is something of a parable of the best of the Africentric outline. We have taken issues and events intended to crush us and defeat our efforts and turned them into incentives to do good. Sullivan is one of our heroes, but there are many others. Among these are Harriet Tubman, fearless leader in the Underground Railroad. More recently, Rosa Parks just sat down in the wrong section on a segregated bus. But if she had not sat down, Martin Luther King Jr. would not have stood up. We must tell such stories to our church assemblies. Our youth need to know these persons and what they were able to do against great odds.

It is not sufficient that we define carefully the terms we have explicated. It is essential that we make them come alive in our collective experience.

Liberation and Reconciliation in Africentric Perspective

These twin perspectives of the gospel have abiding significance. When I introduced them in my first systematic theology on the black experience, I did so almost spontaneously. As I understood the gospel, it was obvious that both liberation and reconciliation are dimensions of the gospel that needed strong affirmation. A student from South

Africa reminded me of their importance in his country. After the election, reconciliation is as important a theme as liberation was before the new South Africa.

First of all, the gospel has both a vertical and horizontal reach. It reaches up to God — or as Karl Barth would say, God reaches down to us. The divine-human encounter is crucial. Horizontally, the gospel reaches out to others. Central to the outlook of King, the gospel is a message of love that reaches out to other humans, even our enemies. Dietrich Bonhoeffer reminds us of the "cost of discipleship" and describes Jesus as "the man for others." In the aspects of love and justice, the gospel is comprehensive — it is concerned with how we relate to God redemptively and at the same time how we reach out to others, ethically.

Second, the gospel that informs our Christian life is at once priestly and prophetic. It seems to me that liberation theologies have majored in the political dimensions of the gospel. Liberation only is always in danger of becoming mainly humanistic. For instance, the *kairos* document that came out of South Africa a few years ago was very influential. The church was described in political terms. It was seen as either endorsing the state or against the state. The document was clear that the church should oppose apartheid. It was a forceful and important message at that time and place. However, the *kairos* document did not give adequate attention to the theological foundations of the church of Jesus Christ or the work of the Holy Spirit. What we had was a theological statement to meet a crisis-liberation thrust from racist oppression. In a similar vein, the early documents out of black theology and Latin America liberation share this emphasis. This focus upon the liberation-political dimension of faith is a strength and a weakness, if we see an either/or position.

By contrast, mainline Protestant theology, especially evangelical theology, majors in the personal or priestly dimension of the gospel. This can easily degenerate into sentimental love on the personal plane and cheap grace as we confront sinful social structures. This does not mean that the priestly dimension of the gospel is unimportant. In fact, it takes on added importance when a group of people is severely oppressed. The church's ministry of healing and consolation is greatly needed when we face structural evils, such as race and gender discrimination. Here the message of Howard Thurman speaks to our need more than the powerful witness of King. Thurman spoke of a Jesus who identified with the "disinherited" and proclaimed a message of healing for those who suffer injustices. He exalted a gospel that contained the balm of Gilead, which makes the wounded whole.

Ron Sider, my colleague who heads Evangelicals for Social Action, has hammered away at what he calls "a one-sided Christianity." I often remind him and other evangelical thinkers that black Christians when left alone have a multidimensional faith. It is holistic, containing a balance between the prophetic and priestly aspects of faith and life. It is natural for us to embrace the disturbing and healing dimensions of the gospel. Moreover, in its Africanness it enfolds all of life here and in the hereafter.

Liberation, properly understood, refers to liberation from oppression. At the same time, it points to being set free from personal sins that lead to physical and spiritual death. Personal salvation and social salvation are both inherent in our understanding of the gospel. Reconciliation is lifted to a higher plane in black theology. It does not mean only personal reconciliation with God. It is not a "soul and Savior" understanding. It also has social implications. God in Christ has reconciled us, but at the same time God through Christ enlists us in a ministry of reconciliation. Because God has mightily redeemed us, we are involved in making life more human for our fellow humans. We are summoned to a caring and sharing life and ministry. Reconciliation with God includes reconciliation with fellow humans.

St. Augustine, the African bishop of Hippo, illustrates how the twin attributes of love and justice are grounded in the nature of God and expressed in the Christian life. Whereas Anders Nygren in his *Agape and Eros* writes concerning an either/or distinction between *Eros* (self-love) and *Agape* (God's love), Augustine exalts self-love as self-respect and God's love as taking the love of self up into the love of God. The love of God (*amor Dei*), which he calls *caritas*, is the source of all love. Even with his strong doctrine of original sin and predestination, he was able to assert that we should love God and do as we please. All genuine love is included in the love of God. To love God enables us to overcome the love of self as selfishness. It also requires us to love others (in them is the same image of God that we have within us). The Christian life is for Augustine "a love triangle," which includes the self, the other, and God. However, all Christian love is grounded in the love of God, or *caritas.*

Caritas applied ethically requires that we affirm our dignity as those created in the image of God. All persons hold their worth as human persons, and this is grounded in God's creative purpose. All have sinned and share a state of fallenness, or separation from God. All are redeemed by the grace of God. All people owe their salvation to the healing cross, the power of the resurrection, and the agency of the Holy Spirit. In this manner, we understand that the gospel liberates us from sin and death and from sinful social structures of oppression. Our ministry is one of liberation and reconciliation through Christ at the witness of the Holy Spirit. All who live the Christian life, regardless of race or ethnicity, are called to witness to a ministry of healing and liberation. In the words of Jesus,

> "The Spirit of the Lord is upon me, because he hath anointed me to preach the gospel to the poor; he hath sent me to preach deliverance to the captives, and recovering of sight to the blind, to set at liberty them that are bruised." (Luke 4:18)

Africentrism/Multiculturalism and Christian Mission

The World Council of Churches (WCC) has launched an ecumenical process to lead their way in contextualizing the gospel in diverse cultures. I have participated in this process, nationally and globally. What the WCC is doing in that regard illustrates concretely the manner in which the mission of Christians from every ethnic and racial (cultural) context can work together for the empowerment of the mission of communities of faith, locally and globally.[14]

My participation in conversations at the Ecumenical and Cultural Institute at Collegeville, Minnesota, and Bossey, Switzerland, has made me aware of the importance of this process at all times and places. In the Bossey consultation, during the summer of 1996, I joined an ecumenical delegation of scholars, pastors, and laypersons with an African American background to share our theology and church traditions with Third World Christians. Among the African Americans were outstanding musicians. Not only did we share our church history and theology, but also we worshipped according to the black church tradition. We shared how our faith informs life and social transformation in our context. The dialogue with persons from other cultures was helpful in affirming our strengths and identifying our weaknesses. This encounter with Christians across denominations and cultures was a source of mutual growth and a new dedication for witness on the part of all who participated. The Collegeville encounter was also powerful. However, it was mainly Eurocentric. The Africentric input was minimal. With a greater balance, the Collegeville-type encounter would be helpful in the United States church community. Africentrism, is therefore, a significant aspect of a multicultural expression of the gospel. I agree with the affirmation of the WCC: "The gospel we proclaim is one, but it necessarily finds expression in a variety of cultural forms. The diversity of cultural expression of the one faith is a rich blessing upon the church, bestowed by the Holy Spirit who leads us into all truth."[15]

While diversity in faith is celebrated, there must always be also the quest for community: "While cultural plurality is a blessing reflecting the richness and diversity of humankind, any Christian witness which does not promote community is a counter-sign of the Gospel."[16] There needs, therefore, to be a constant effort to find a balance between full acceptance of one's own heritage (culture) and meaningful exchanges with people (believers) of other denominations and heritages in the interest of community. This will require dialogue on ideas and beliefs and cooperation in facing issues and taking action on matters that are cross-cultural. A sense of equality, compassion, fellow-feeling, justice, and mutual respect are necessary to forge a genuine community in this situation.

Without being aware of the present Africentric movement, I opened the door to this rich possibility in my *Liberation and Reconciliation* (1971). Standing between King's nonviolent integrationist view and the black power separatist outlook, I spoke of reconciliation between equals only. There I discussed interracial fellowship and cooperation between black and white Christians.[17]

In concrete terms, this would mean that African American Christians would take their cultural heritage into account in lifestyle and worship. They would even celebrate this heritage. At the same time, European Americans, Hispanics, Asians, and others would likewise. However, when they joined in a community of worship or action, they would do so in the spirit of mutual respect around the "one gospel." The possibility for interracial and interethnic fellowship would still exist. This, however, would require a great deal of maturity in all concerned. Common study, much fellowship, and spiritual growth would need to proceed this worthy Christian goal. Common worship, fellowship, and action would be a good foundation for Africentrism and multiculturalism to embrace each other in Christian mission in cross-cultural perspective. In this manner, African American Christians may join all other Christians in a common mission in the spirit of the Lord of the church when he prayed "that they all may be one" (John 17:21).

Notes

1. Nathan Glazer speaks of a "multicultural explosion" in *We Are All Multiculturalists Now* (Cambridge, Mass.: Harvard University Press, 1997), 1.

2. Deb Riechmann (Associated Press), "Report: Racial Divide Widens," *The Herald-Sun* (Durham, N.C.), March 1, 1998, A1; the report is "The Millennium Breach."

3. Ibid.

4. Ibid., A2.

5. Molefi Kete Asante, "The Painful Demise of Eurocentrism," *The World and I* (April 1992), 309.

6. Ibid.

7. Ibid.

8. Ibid.

9. Ibid., 310.

10. Ibid., 311.

11. Ibid.

12. Ibid., 12. I will not repeat the discussion between Schlesinger and Asante on the blackness of ancient Egyptians.

13. Ibid., 313–17.

14. The purpose of this three-year conversion is described in several releases. Among them is "An Invitation to Participate in the WCC Study Process on Gospel and Cultures." The "One Gospel Many Cultures" process is treated in pamphlets, resource packets for leaders, and videotapes. Guidelines for study groups are available.

15. WCC Fifth World Conference on Faith and Order, 1993. Quoted in *A Study Project on Gospel and Culture in the U.S.*, U.S. Office of WCC, 8.

16. "One Gospel Many Cultures," pamphlet, 1997.

17. This discussion is now found in *Liberation and Reconciliation, 2nd edition* (Maryknoll, N.Y.: Orbis Books, 1994), 60–61.